. . . a teacher's guide to accompany

WRITE SOURCE®

GREAT SOURCE EDUCATION GROUP
a Houghton Mifflin Company
Wilmington, Massachusetts

About the Teacher's Guide

It's important for you to know a few things about your *Writers Express Teacher's Guide* before you begin to use it.

Previewing ● The opening section provides a quick tour of the handbook to help you become familiar with its basic features. The next section—"Getting Started"—contains guidelines and reproducible activity sheets that you can use to introduce the handbook to your students.

Planning ● "Using the Student Handbook" provides a variety of ideas for planning instruction. The next three sections contain summaries for all of the handbook chapters related to writing and learning skills. The "Handbook Minilessons" section contains a variety of activities to use along with the handbook. (One minilesson is provided for each handbook chapter.)

Managing ● "Evaluating/Assessing/Monitoring" offers suggestions for evaluating writing, basic-skills instruction, and extended units. Also included in this section is valuable information related to peer conferencing and portfolio assessment.

Supplementing ● The final sections in the *Teacher's Guide* serve as a resource for improving instruction with the handbook. "Reading-Writing Connection" lists high-interest trade books related to major chapters in the handbook. These lists can help when planning extended units. The "Bibliography" section lists additional resources for each chapter, which may also help during planning. Finally, "Language Series Overview" highlights the coordinating program for grades 4 and 5.

Authors: Pat Sebranek and Dave Kemper

Printed in the United States of America

International Standard Book Number: 0-669-38835-1

7 8 9 10 -HLG- 00 99 98

What You'll Find Inside

Table of Contents

Writers Express Student Handbook

Writers Express serves as the perfect language handbook for grades 4 and 5, one that will help your students improve their ability **to write** (prewriting through proofreading), **to think** (creatively, logically, and clearly), and **to learn** (in the classroom, in small groups, independently). This quick tour will highlight the handbook's major points of interest.

A Quick Tour of ***Writers Express***

1

The Process of Writing ● Students will use this section of the handbook to answer their questions about writing, from selecting a subject to proofreading a final draft.

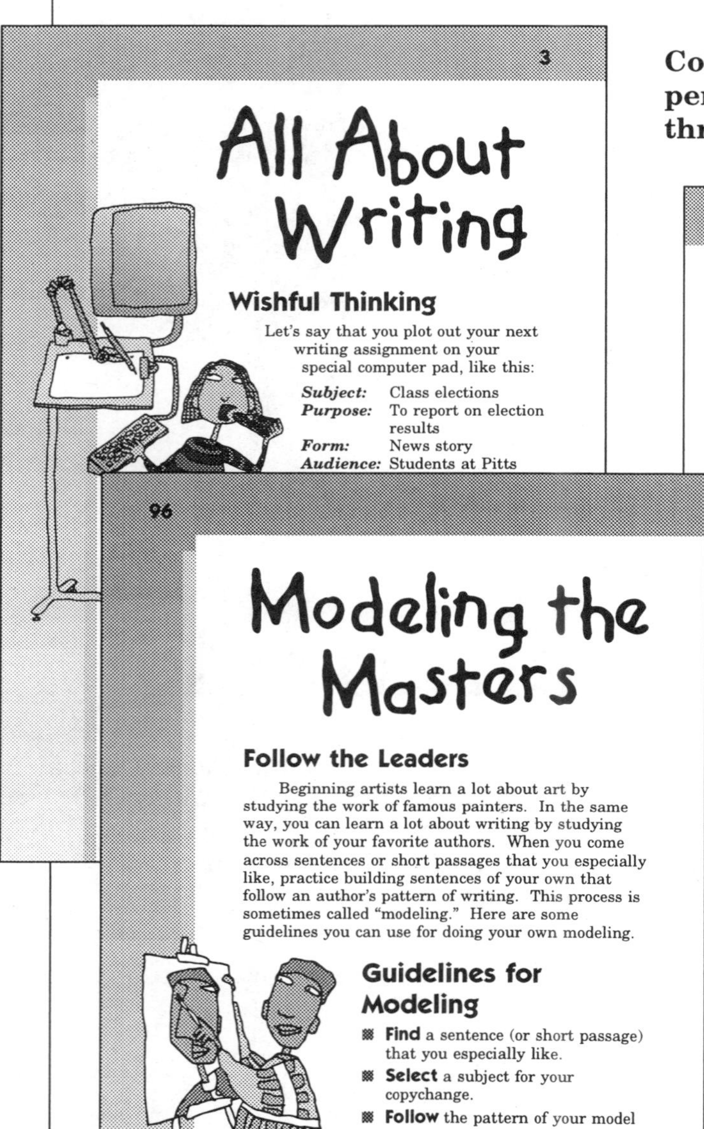

3

All About Writing

Wishful Thinking

Let's say that you plot out your next writing assignment on your special computer pad, like this:

Subject: Class elections
Purpose: To report on election results
Form: News story
Audience: Students at Pitts

96

Modeling the Masters

Follow the Leaders

Beginning artists learn a lot about art by studying the work of famous painters. In the same way, you can learn a lot about writing by studying the work of your favorite authors. When you come across sentences or short passages that you especially like, practice building sentences of your own that follow an author's pattern of writing. This process is sometimes called "modeling." Here are some guidelines you can use for doing your own modeling.

Guidelines for Modeling

- **Find** a sentence (or short passage) that you especially like.
- **Select** a subject for your copychange.
- **Follow** the pattern of your model sentences as you write about your subject.
- **Build** your sentence one small section at a time.
- **Review** your work, and change any parts that seem confusing or unclear.

Colorful illustrations and a personal tone are used throughout *Writers Express*.

6 All About Writing

The Writing Process in Action

These two pages provide a basic look at the writing process in action. You will find this information helpful if you have never used the writing process before or if you would like a general guide to follow when you write.

PREWRITING

Prewriting means getting ready to write. Follow these basic steps during prewriting:

- **Select** a subject that really interests you.
- **Collect** details about your subject if you don't know a lot about it.
- **Plan** what you want to say about your subject (the main idea of your writing) and how you want to say it (the form of your writing).

WRITING THE FIRST DRAFT

Once you've collected your thoughts about your subject, write the first draft of your paper.

- **Write** this draft freely, getting *all* of your ideas on paper.
- **Imagine** that you are talking to a group of friends.
- **Let** your prewriting and planning be your guide as you write.

Step-by-step instructions, helpful guidelines, and checklists make information easy to find and use.

2 The Forms of Writing

The Forms of Writing • When students are ready to start a personal journal, or write a poem, or create a tall tale, this is the section to turn to.

Writing in Journals 109

Dialogue Journal

In this second sample, a student and teacher carry on a conversation about a book.

Feb.3

Dear Susan,

That part in Mrs. Frankweiler where the kids are hiding in the bathroom made me think of the time I hid from my mom in K-Mart. I didn't want to go home, so I hid behind the shower curtains. She was so mad! I thought of this because my heart was beating really fast whenever Mom got close to me, like the kids' hearts in the book. (Hey, when does your heart beat fast?)

Sincerely,
Mrs. N

Dear Mrs.

Thank
your moth
beats fast
(2) when
and (3)
math prob
are! (1

Your frie
Susan

124 Writing Newspaper Stories

The Parts of a Reporter

142

Writing Business Letters

When You Mean Business

A **business letter** is different from a letter you write to an aunt in another city or to a pen pal in another country. It looks and sounds more business-like and focuses on only one subject.

You may write a business letter for different reasons:

- **when you need information** (*a letter of request*),
- **when you have a problem with something you ordered** (*a letter of complaint*),
- **or when you have a problem with a situation in your city or school** (*a letter to an editor or official*).

But no matter what type of business letter you write, you should follow the guidelines given in this chapter. Your letters will bring better results if you do them right. Pay special attention to the sample letter on page 145.

Writers Express **addresses many forms of writing, from scientific observation reports to songs.**

3 The Tools of Learning

● If your students' study, reading, or test-taking skills could use a little pumping up, have them turn to "The Tools of Learning."

248 Reading Pictures

➤ Diagrams

A **diagram** is like a map, but instead of a place, it shows . . . almost anything! You could draw a diagram of a bicycle, a computer, or the bones in the human hand.

Bones of the Hand
Right hand (palm up)
Phalanges Metacarpals Carpals
Ulna
Radius

Picture Diagram ● A picture diagram is a drawing that shows how something is put together, how the parts relate to one another, or how the thing works. Diagrams may leave out some parts, showing only what you need to learn. This diagram of a hand leaves out the skin and muscles so that you can see the bones.

Line Diagram ● In a way, line diagrams are like symbols: They can show something that you can't really see. For example, a family tree is a diagram of how your relatives are related. It helps you get a picture of where everybody fits, but your parents aren't really hanging over yo

FATHER
SISTER ME

THINK IT OVER

If a diagr things m that pictu top to bot clues like

255

Building Vocabulary Skills

Becoming More Wordwise

Think of your vocabulary as all the words you are able to use. These are the words you use when you are reading, writing, and talking. They are the tools in your language tool kit. The more tools you have, the better you will be able to think and communicate.

Smarten Up!

Having more words at your command also helps you become a better listener and reader. Let's say you hear this comment: "Jim *donated* $10 to the group." By knowing what ted" means, you would know that Jim does not to get his money back. Then you hear, "Carlos 10 to the group." By knowing what "lent" means, ould know Carlos expects to get his money back. o how can you "smarten up" and become a listener and reader? Just read (and follow) the stions given in this chapter.

320 Completing Assignments

Managing Your Time

Are you a *procrastinator*? Do you sometimes put off doing things that you should do? Well, the truth is, we all procrastinate at times. But if you put things off all the time, then you need to learn about time management.

Steps in the Process

1 Make a daily list. Write down things you *need* to do today, perhaps in a small spiral notebook. Number your "To Do" list from the most important to the least important, and cross each one off as you complete it.

2 Keep a weekly schedule. A weekly planner shows you what you have to do during the week. It helps you plan your study time and your fun time. Use the following model or design your own.

WEEKLY PLANNER

Day	Assignment	Due Date	Activities	Study Time	Fun Time
Monday					
Tuesday					

Figure out what time of the day you think and work best. Use this time for your toughest assignments and most important work.

3 Turn big jobs into little ones. When you have a big assignment to do, it can seem really overwhelming. One way to make it seem easier is to turn it into smaller jobs. Figure out how many days you have to complete the assignment, and how much you need to do each day. Working 15 minutes a day for two weeks beats two or three hours of work the night before your project is due.

***Writers Express* contains lots of easy-to-use ideas for making all aspects of language and learning active, enjoyable, and meaningful.**

4 The Proofreader's Guide

The Proofreader's Guide • Whenever students have a question about punctuation, spelling, or capitalization, here's where they can "Check It Out!"

This guide to spelling, usage, punctuation, and capitalization answers all your students' proofreading questions.

USING THE RIGHT WORD

You will want to use "the right words" whenever you write. This section will help you do just that. Begin by looking over the commonly misused words on the next eight pages. Then, whenever you have a question about which word is the *right* word, come back to this section for help. P.S. Remember to look for your word in a dictionary if you don't find it here.

a, an	I played a joke on my dad. (*A is used before words beginning with a consonant sound.*) I placed an ugly rubber fish under his pillow. (*An is used before words beginning with a vowel sound.*)
accept, except	Please ***accept*** (receive) my apology. Everyone else has ***except*** (other than) you.
affect, effect	Jorge's funny face ***affected*** the whole class. (***Affect*** *is always a verb meaning "to influence."*) The ***effect*** (result) was a class full of giggling students.
...d, aloud	We are ***allowed*** (permitted) to read to partners in class. But we may not read ***aloud*** in the library.
... lot	

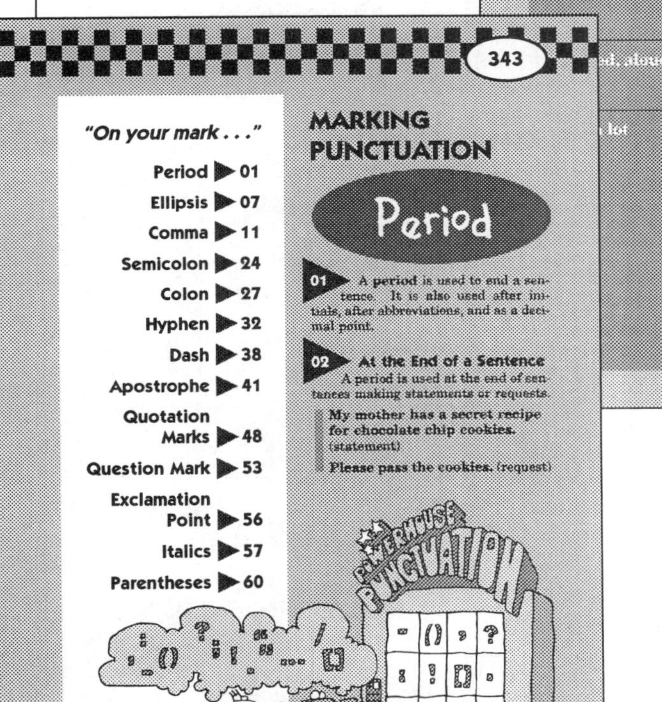

343

"On your mark . . ."

Period ▶ 01
Ellipsis ▶ 07
Comma ▶ 11
Semicolon ▶ 24
Colon ▶ 27
Hyphen ▶ 32
Dash ▶ 38
Apostrophe ▶ 41
Quotation Marks ▶ 48
Question Mark ▶ 53
Exclamation Point ▶ 56
Italics ▶ 57
Parentheses ▶ 60

MARKING PUNCTUATION

Period

01 A period is used to end a sentence. It is also used after initials, after abbreviations, and as a decimal point.

02 **At the End of a Sentence**
A period is used at the end of sentences making statements or requests.

My mother has a secret recipe for chocolate chip cookies. (statement)
Please pass the cookies. (request)

358

CHECKING YOUR SPELLING

1. You'll need to be patient. **Learning to become a good speller takes time.**
2. **Check your spelling** by using a dictionary or list of commonly misspelled words (like the list which follows).
3. **Check a dictionary for the correct pronunciation** of each word you are trying to spell. Knowing how to pronounce a word will help you remember how to spell it.
4. Also **look up the meaning** of each word. (Knowing how to spell a word is of little use if you don't know what it means.)
5. **Practice seeing the word in your mind's eye.** Look away from the dictionary page and write the word on a piece of paper. Check the spelling in the dictionary. Repeat this process until you can spell the word correctly.
6. **Make a spelling dictionary.** Include any words you misspell in a special notebook. (***SEE*** page 271.)

Just as you must watch and practice to become a better basketball player, you must read and write to become a better speller.

A

about, above, absent, accept, accident, accompany, accurate, ache, achieve, across, actual, address, adventure, advertisement, advise

afraid, after, against, agreement, allowance, all right, almost, alone, along, a lot, already, although, always, American, among, amount, ancient

angel, angle, animal, anniversary, anonymous, another, answer, anybody, apartment, apologize, application, appreciate, April, aren't, argument, arithmetic, around

arrival, article, artificial, athlete, athletic, attention, attitude, attractive, audience, August, aunt, author, automobile, autumn, avenue, awful, awhile

5 The Student Almanac

The Student Almanac ● Full-color maps, a historical time line, the metric system—*Writers Express* is truly an all-school handbook!

"The Student Almanac" contains information useful for math, science, and social studies classes.

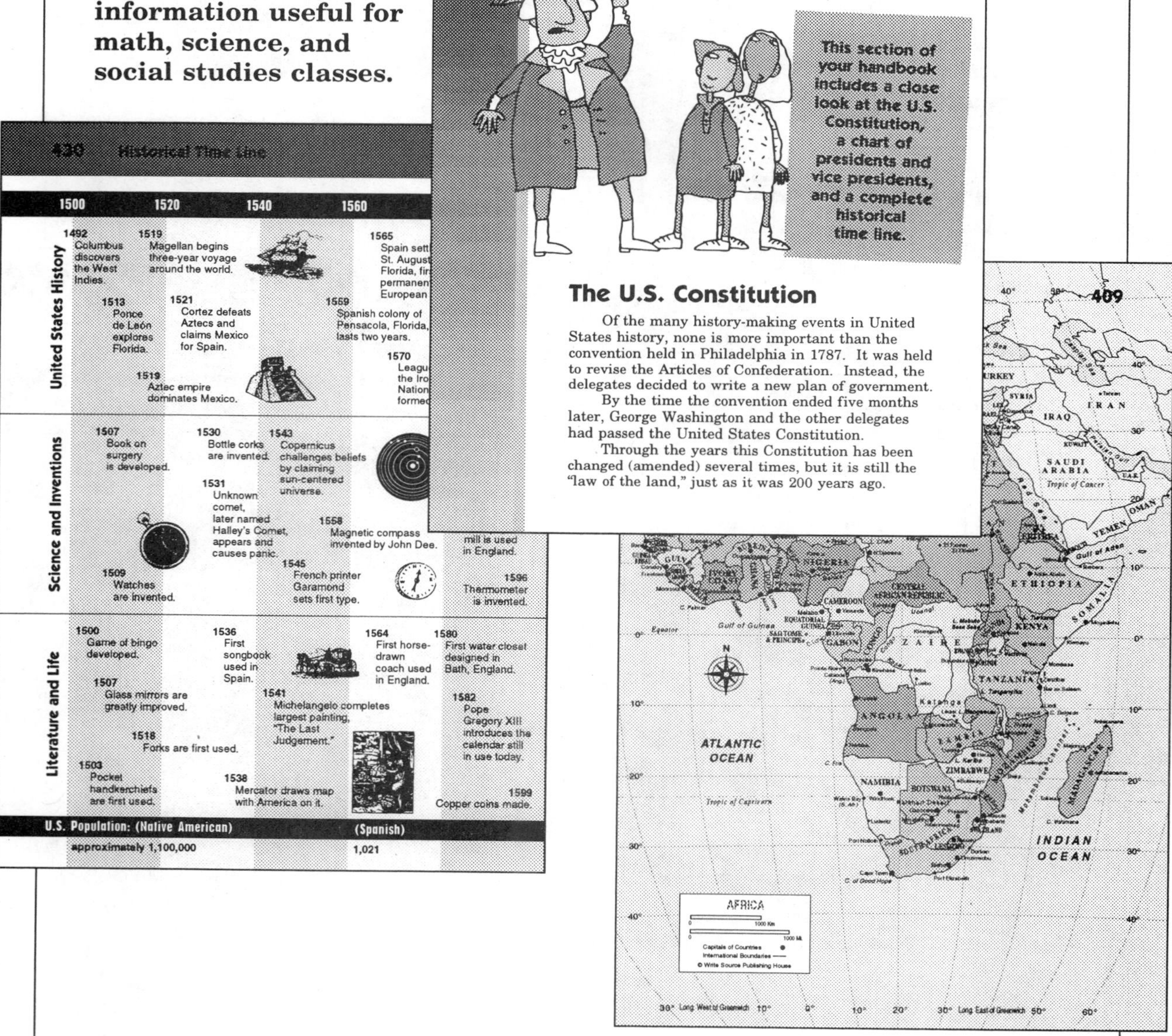
494

History in the Making

This section of your handbook includes a close look at the U.S. Constitution, a chart of presidents and vice presidents, and a complete historical time line.

The U.S. Constitution

Of the many history-making events in United States history, none is more important than the convention held in Philadelphia in 1787. It was held to revise the Articles of Confederation. Instead, the delegates decided to write a new plan of government.

By the time the convention ended five months later, George Washington and the other delegates had passed the United States Constitution.

Through the years this Constitution has been changed (amended) several times, but it is still the "law of the land," just as it was 200 years ago.

430 Historical Time Line

1500 1520 1540 1560

United States History

1492 Columbus discovers the West Indies.

1519 Magellan begins three-year voyage around the world.

1565 Spain sett... St. August... Florida, fir... permanen... European...

1513 Ponce de León explores Florida.

1521 Cortez defeats Aztecs and claims Mexico for Spain.

1559 Spanish colony of Pensacola, Florida, lasts two years.

1570 Leagu... the Iro... Nation... formed

1519 Aztec empire dominates Mexico.

Science and Inventions

1507 Book on surgery is developed.

1530 Bottle corks are invented.

1543 Copernicus challenges beliefs by claiming sun-centered universe.

1531 Unknown comet, later named Halley's Comet, appears and causes panic.

1558 Magnetic compass invented by John Dee.

mill is used in England.

1545 French printer Garamond sets first type.

1509 Watches are invented.

1596 Thermometer is invented.

Literature and Life

1500 Game of bingo developed.

1536 First songbook used in Spain.

1564 First horse-drawn coach used in England.

1580 First water closet designed in Bath, England.

1507 Glass mirrors are greatly improved.

1541 Michelangelo completes largest painting, "The Last Judgement."

1582 Pope Gregory XIII introduces the calendar still in use today.

1518 Forks are first used.

1503 Pocket handkerchiefs are first used.

1538 Mercator draws map with America on it.

1599 Copper coins made.

U.S. Population: (Native American) approximately 1,100,000

(Spanish) 1,021

409

Getting Started Activities

Writers Express was developed by experienced teachers and writers for intermediate students. More than anything else, we wanted to put together a handbook that students would find very helpful and enjoyable to use. Over the past several years, teachers have told us what they like best about our other handbooks, and what they do when the book is first put into the hands of their students.

Many of their suggestions, plus some of our own, are contained in this section of your *Teacher's Guide*. Of special interest to you will be the suggested sequences of activities (page 11) for introducing the handbook to your students and the reproducible activity sheets on pages 12-17.

Start-Up Ideas

Handbook Design

Before you even hand out *Writers Express,* ask students what they would put into an all-purpose student handbook if they were in charge of designing one. (They may come up with ideas like topics for writing, tips for taking a test, and so on.) List their suggestions on the board or on an overhead. Then hand out *Writers Express,* and ask students to review the handbook, noting how it matches up to the list on the board. (Have students share the results of their review.)

Scavenger Hunts

One popular way to help students get to know the handbook is to create scavenger hunts, which basically ask students to find a random list of items in *Writers Express*. (Some answers should be fairly obvious, some less so.) You can also use one or more of the reproducible activity sheets we have provided to send your students on scavenger hunts or related tasks. (See pages 12-17 in this section.)

One Point of Interest

Give your students the following assignment: Find one page, one short section, one set of guidelines, one illustration, one model, or one chart you think is interesting, entertaining, stimulating, valuable, etc. Students should prepare to share their discoveries with members of their discussion group or with the entire class.

Five W's & H

Have students develop *who, what, when, where, why,* and *how* questions from *Writers Express*. Students should then exchange questions with a partner and search for answers in the handbook. Upon completion, partners should read and react to each other's answers.

Example questions:

Who *often tells the best family stories?*

What *is the first step in the writing process?*

A Variation: Small groups or teams of students could develop questions and compete in a handbook-search contest.

Quotable Quotes

Ask each student to find one quote in *Writers Express* that he or she especially likes. Afterward, have students discuss the reasons for their selections.

All-School Handbook

Have students list all of their subjects (math, science, etc.) along the left-hand margin of a piece of paper. They should skip two lines between each subject. Then ask students to identify two pieces of information—chapters, pages, checklists, and the like—in *Writers Express* that would help them in each subject. Have students share the results of their work.

Wall Charts

Have small groups of students design wall charts based on helpful checklists or guidelines included in *Writers Express*. (The guidelines for writing in a journal on page 106 of the handbook might be an example.) Display the finished products in your classroom as well as in other classrooms.

Minilessons

Have students—individually or in pairs—prepare minilessons to go along with the proofreader's guide in *Writers Express* (pages 343-387). These minilessons should be presented to the class on a regular basis.

Chapter Reviews

As an extended activity, ask pairs of students to select one chapter in *Writers Express* to review for the rest of the class. Their reviews should highlight three or four parts of the chapter they really like and find helpful.

Your First Week with the Handbook

DAY 1	Distribute copies of *Writers Express,* and give your students a few minutes to preview the handbook. Have them share first impressions. Then discuss how the handbook is organized, referring students to both the table of contents and the index. To help students get to know the handbook, ask them to work on the activity sheet "Scavenger Hunt" (A or B) or on one of the other getting-started activities on pages 12-17.
DAY 2	Provide time at the beginning of the class period for students to complete their work on the scavenger hunt. Then discuss the results of their work. (See the answer key on page 18 or page 19.) For the rest of the class period, ask students to complete the "One Point of Interest" activity on page 9.
DAY 3	Have students share their points of interest in small groups or with the entire class. To help students understand that *Writers Express* deals with all areas of language learning, assign the activity sheet "Your Complete Language Guide" on page 16.
DAY 4	Have students share the results of their work using the follow-up at the bottom of the language guide activity sheet on page 16. Read "Why Write?" (pages x-xi in *Writers Express*) aloud to the students. Afterward, ask students to think of the most important, meaningful, or satisfying pieces of writing they have completed in school or on their own. (You may want to share some of your own important or meaningful writing experiences to prompt their thinking.) As your students work on this activity, they will be forming their own answers to the "Why Write?" question.
DAY 5	Read pages 3-5 of "All About Writing" (in *Writers Express*) with your students as an introduction to the writing process. Then distribute copies of the "Get Ready, Get Set, Go!" activity sheet (page 14) for students to work on. This sheet will help students see how information about the writing process and the forms of writing is organized in *Writers Express.* (Students should have time on the next school day to complete and share their work.)

Continue reading and sharing different parts of the handbook from week to week. Also, implement the other getting-started activities on a regular basis.

Name ___

Scavenger Hunt A

DIRECTIONS: **Using the table of contents in your handbook, write down the *page number* you would turn to if you were looking for the following types of information.**

1. You want to know how to publish a piece of writing. ______
2. You are going to write a news story for your class newspaper. ______
3. You could use help studying for an important test. ______
4. You wonder where to put the commas when writing a date. ______
5. You want to know which U.S. president served the longest time. ______

DIRECTIONS: **Now, using the handbook index, follow the directions listed below.**

6. Find a checklist for editing and proofreading your writing.

   page number: ______

   What is one thing you should check for?

   ______

7. Find information about alliteration. page number: ______

   What example is given? ______

8. Find information about graphs. page numbers: ______

   Name one type of graph. ______

9. Find a list of greetings in foreign languages. page number: ______

   How would you say "good-bye" in Thai? ______

10. Find a map of Asia. page number: ______

    Name one country that borders India. ______

    ______

Name ______________________________

Scavenger Hunt B

DIRECTIONS: Using the table of contents in your handbook, write down the *page number* you would turn to if you were looking for the following types of information.

1. You want to combine some shorter sentences in one of your papers. ______
2. You need to know how to summarize a magazine article you are reading for science class. ______
3. You want to become a better reader. ______
4. You want to use the right word—*to, too,* or *two*. ______
5. You're considering a new pet and wonder how long rabbits live. ______

DIRECTIONS: Now, using the handbook index, follow the directions listed below.

6. Find information about the parts of a business letter. page number: ______

   What part includes the sender's address? ______________________________
7. Find a checklist of listening skills. page number: ______

   What is the first thing you should do to improve your listening?

   ____
8. Find information about television viewing. page numbers: ______________

   On average, how many hours of TV do we watch each week? ____________
9. Find information about punctuating titles. page numbers: ______________

   What punctuation is used for the title of a song? ______________________
10. Find information about the planets. page numbers: ____________________

    How far is Earth from the sun? ______________________________

Name

Get Ready, Get Set, Go!

DIRECTIONS: **As you follow the directions below, you will learn about the first two sections in the handbook: "The Process of Writing" and "The Forms of Writing."**

1. Turn to page 5 and read about the five steps in the writing process. What are the first and last steps?

2. Take a look at page 18. What does a writer collect in a portfolio?

3. Read Charles Vodak's story (page 47). What title would you give this story?

4. Review pages 72-73 in the essay section. Name two things an essay can do.

5. Study page 86. What are the two basic parts of a sentence?

6. Look at the parts of a newspaper story on page 128. What is a byline?

7. Turn to the section on tall tales (page 160). What is the name of the character whose picture is on this page?

8. Introduce yourself to Amanda Lowe on page 164. She has a problem that could be the starting point for a realistic story. What is her problem?

9. Read the report on page 221. Identify the most surprising fact you learned about the subject.

Name

A Quick Tour

DIRECTIONS: As you follow the directions below, you will learn about the last three sections in the handbook: "The Tools of Learning," "Proofreader's Guide," and "The Student Almanac."

1. Identify two strategies for building your vocabulary (page 256).

2. Study page 309 to learn about thinking clearly. Find out the difference between a fact and an opinion. Then write one *fact* about *Writers Express*.

3. Review the information about taking an essay test on page 331. Then identify the first step in answering an essay-test question.

4. Write your own address in a sentence, using commas in the right places (page 345).

   My address is

5. Check out the section on apostrophes (page 349) to find out what the word "o'clock" is short for and write it here.

6. Pretend you work at a Taco Bell restaurant and have an order for more than one *burrito*. How would you write the plural of *burrito* (page 355)?

7. Decide if you write on stationary or stationery (page 368).

8. List one proper and two common nouns that you see on this activity sheet (page 375).

9. Study the United States map (page 405). Identify the state capital of Ohio.

Name

Your Complete Language Guide

Writers Express can help you in *all* of these areas.

DIRECTIONS: **Complete the chart below by listing two specific chapters, pages, or checklists in the handbook that can help you become a better writer, reader, speaker, and so on. One space has been filled in to get you started.**

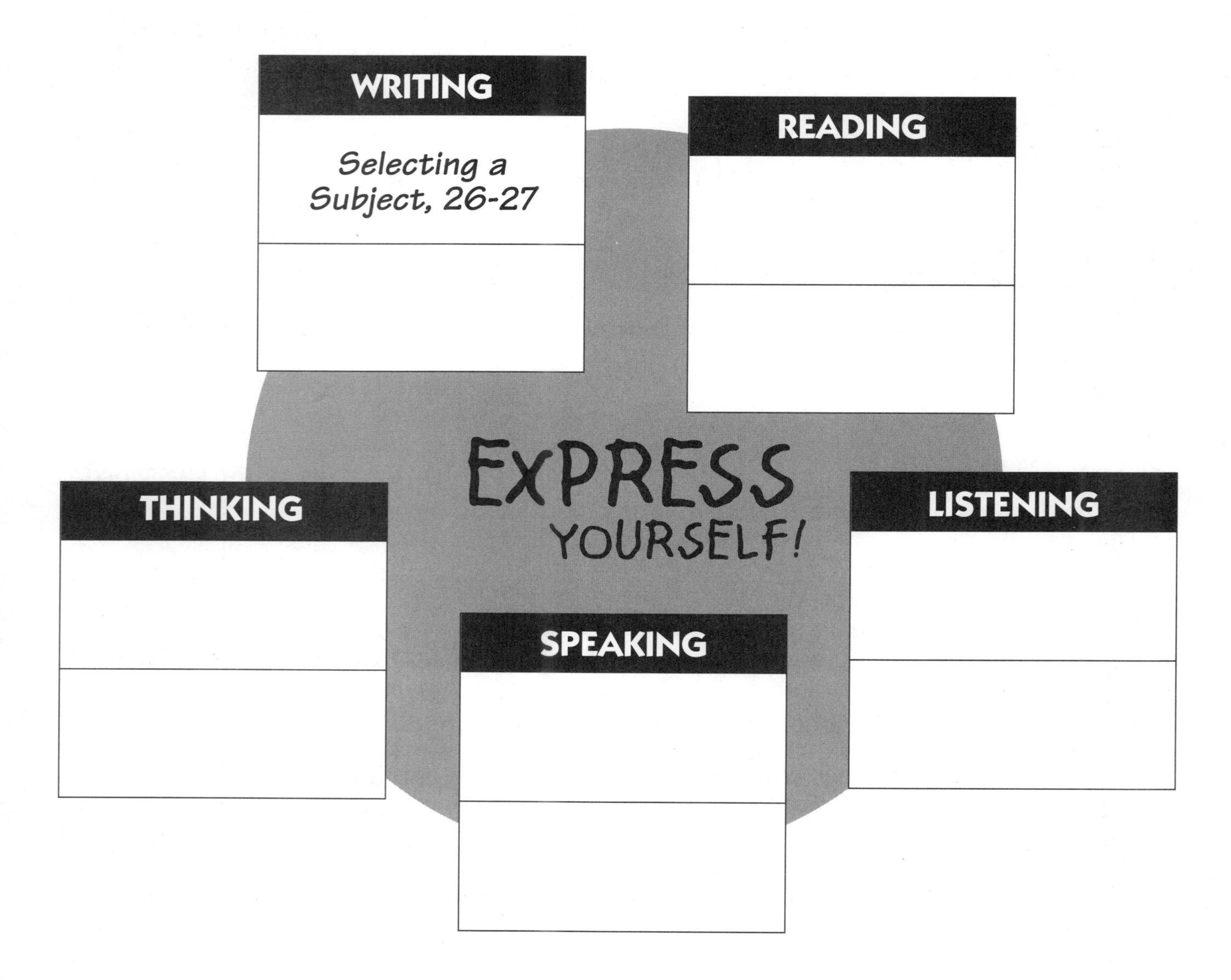

The Next Step ● After filling in all of these spaces, share your work with a classmate. Give a reason for each one of your choices.

Name

Getting to Know *Writers Express*

DIRECTIONS: To complete this chart, you will have to find words from six different lists in *Writers Express*. (Use the index to find each list.) Make sure that the words you select begin with the letters in the left-hand column, and make sure that you spell these words correctly. (Two words have been filled in for you.)

	Commonly Misspelled Words (See "Spelling")	Writing Terms	Thinking and Writing Guidelines	Usage and Commonly Misused Words	Countries I Have Never Seen (See "Maps")	Forms of Writing
E	*electricity*	*editing*				

EXPRESS YOURSELF!

P						
R						
E						
S						
S						

Name

Scavenger Hunt A

DIRECTIONS: Using the table of contents in your handbook, write down the *page number* you would turn to if you were looking for the following types of information.

1. You want to know how to publish a piece of writing. 54
2. You are going to write a news story for your class newspaper. 123
3. You could use help studying for an important test. 328
4. You wonder where to put the commas when writing a date. 345
5. You want to know which U.S. president served the longest time. 428

DIRECTIONS: Now, using the handbook index, follow the directions listed below.

6. Find a checklist for editing and proofreading your writing.

   page number: 53

   What is one thing you should check for?

   sentence structure, punctuation, capitalization, usage, or spelling

7. Find information about alliteration. page number: 183

   What example is given? *dance, dare, and drop*

8. Find information about graphs. page numbers: 249-251

   Name one type of graph. *bar graph, line graph, or pie graph*

9. Find a list of greetings in foreign languages. page number: 392

   How would you say "good-bye" in Thai? *la kone na ka*

10. Find a map of Asia. page number: 411

    Name one country that borders India. *Pakistan, China, Nepal, Bhutan, Bangladesh, or Myanmar*

Name ______________________________

Scavenger Hunt B

DIRECTIONS: Using the table of contents in your handbook, write down the *page number* you would turn to if you were looking for the following types of information.

1. You want to combine some shorter sentences in one of your papers. 90
2. You need to know how to summarize a magazine article you are reading for science class. 216
3. You want to become a better reader. 237
4. You want to use the right word—*to, too,* or *two*. 362 or 369
5. You're considering a new pet and wonder how long rabbits live. 393

DIRECTIONS: Now, using the handbook index, follow the directions listed below.

6. Find information about the parts of a business letter. page number: 144

   What part includes the sender's address? the heading
7. Find a checklist of listening skills. page number: 293

   What is the first thing you should do to improve your listening?

   Listen with a good attitude.
8. Find information about television viewing. page numbers: 288-291

   On average, how many hours of TV do we watch each week? 26
9. Find information about punctuating titles. page numbers: 350-351

   What punctuation is used for the title of a song? quotation marks
10. Find information about the planets. page numbers: 398-399

    How far is Earth from the sun? 92.96 million miles

Name

Get Ready, Get Set, Go!

DIRECTIONS: As you follow the directions below, you will learn about the first two sections in the handbook: "The Process of Writing" and "The Forms of Writing."

1. Turn to page 5 and read about the five steps in the writing process. What are the first and last steps?

   prewriting and publishing

2. Take a look at page 18. What does a writer collect in a portfolio?

   his or her writing work

3. Read Charles Vodak's story (page 47). What title would you give this story?

   (Answers will vary.)

4. Review pages 72-73 in the essay section. Name two things an essay can do.

   present information, share a strong opinion, or make everyone think

5. Study page 86. What are the two basic parts of a sentence?

   the subject and the verb

6. Look at the parts of a newspaper story on page 128. What is a byline?

   the name of the writer of a story

7. Turn to the section on tall tales (page 160). What is the name of the character whose picture is on this page?

   Daniel Boone

8. Introduce yourself to Amanda Lowe on page 164. She has a problem that could be the starting point for a realistic story. What is her problem?

   She is very short.

9. Read the report on page 221. Identify the most surprising fact you learned about the subject.

   (Answers will vary.)

Name

A Quick Tour

DIRECTIONS: **As you follow the directions below, you will learn about the last three sections in the handbook: "The Tools of Learning," "Proofreader's Guide," and "The Student Almanac."**

1. Identify two strategies for building your vocabulary (page 256).

   read, use context clues, keep a vocabulary notebook

2. Study page 309 to learn about thinking clearly. Find out the difference between a fact and an opinion. Then write one *fact* about *Writers Express*.

   (Answers will vary.)

3. Review the information about taking an essay test on page 331. Then identify the first step in answering an essay-test question.

   Reword the question.

4. Write your own address in a sentence, using commas in the right places (page 345).

   My address is *(Answers will vary.)*

5. Check out the section on apostrophes (page 349) to find out what the word "o'clock" is short for and write it here.

   of the clock

6. Pretend you work at a Taco Bell restaurant and have an order for more than one *burrito*. How would you write the plural of *burrito* (page 355)?

   burritos

7. Decide if you write on stationary or stationery (page 368).

   stationery

8. List one proper and two common nouns that you see on this activity sheet (page 375).

   (Answers will vary.)

9. Study the United States map (page 405). Identify the state capital of Ohio.

   Columbus

Name

Your Complete Language Guide

Writers Express can help you in *all* of these areas.

DIRECTIONS: **Complete the chart below by listing two specific chapters, pages, or checklists in the handbook that can help you become a better writer, reader, speaker, and so on. One space has been filled in to get you started.**

(Answers will vary.)

EXPRESS YOURSELF!

WRITING
Selecting a Subject, 26-27
A Basic Writing Guide, 12-15

READING
Using Reading Strategies, 237-245
Using context clues, 256

THINKING
Getting Organized 295-299
Guidelines for Thinking and Writing 307

SPEAKING
The Steps in the Process, 276
Five Performance Tips, 286

LISTENING
Good Listener Checklist, 293
Suggestions for Listeners, 44

The Next Step ● After filling in all of these spaces, share your work with a classmate. Give a reason for each one of your choices.

Name

Getting to Know Writers Express

DIRECTIONS: To complete this chart, you will have to find words from six different lists in *Writers Express*. (Use the index to find each list.) Make sure that the words you select begin with the letters in the left-hand column, and make sure that you spell these words correctly. (Two words have been filled in for you.)

(Answers will vary.)

	Commonly Misspelled Words (See "Spelling")	Writing Terms	Thinking and Writing Guidelines	Usage and Commonly Misused Words	Countries I Have Never Seen (See "Maps")	Forms of Writing
E	*electricity*	*editing*	*explain*	*eye*	*Ecuador*	*E-mail*

EXPRESS YOURSELF!

P	*package*	*pun*	*predict*	*pore*	*Portugal*	*poems*
R	*receive*	*revising*	*rate*	*raise*	*Rwanda*	*reports*
E	*Easter*	*exposition*	*evaluate*	*except*	*Ethiopia*	*editorials*
S	*shoes*	*simile*	*show*	*steal*	*Serbia*	*slogans*
S	*Sunday*	*style*	*select*	*sew*	*Syria*	*songs*

Conducting Minilessons

DIRECTIONS: **Conduct minilessons on a regular basis to give your students practice using *Writers Express*. Use the samples below as a guide when you design your own minilessons.**

That's so basic! . . . . *Using the Basics of Life Checklist*

Let's say, as a writing assignment, you've been asked to explain how to do or make something. USE the guidelines on **page 27** in *Writers Express,* and LIST at least three subjects you could write about. (Share the results of your work.)

Follow a Leader . . . . *Modeling a Professional Writer*

PRACTICE writing sentences modeled after two sentences (or short passages) in one of your favorite books. USE the guidelines and examples on **pages 96-97** in your handbook to help you complete your work. (Share your results.)

First Feelings . . . . . . *Writing in a Reader Response Journal*

LEARN about reader response journals on **page 137** in *Writers Express*. Then WRITE four or five journal entries for the next book you read, using the "Ideas for Responding" section as your guide. Try to write at least eight or nine lines each time you write. (Share the results of your work.)

Did you say "Quill"? . . . . . *Using the KWL Reading Strategy*

LEARN about the KWL reading strategy on **page 242** in *Writers Express*. Then USE the strategy as you read any chapter in the handbook. (Share the results of your work.)

Study Time and Fun Time . . . . . *Keeping a Weekly Schedule*

PLAN your study time and fun time for the next week using the "Weekly Planner" chart on **page 320** in your handbook as your guide. After the week is over, WRITE a journal entry exploring how the planner worked for you. (Share the results of your work.)

Using the Student Handbook

Teachers often ask how *Writers Express* can be used in their classrooms. The answer to that question is easy. Teachers should think of *Writers Express* as their teacher's aide, on hand to help students at all times—during class, throughout the school day, and later at home—with their writing, reading, and learning. The pages that follow preview the wide range of material included in the five major sections of the handbook and offer suggestions for using this material. (Note: The first page is a framework listing the forms of writing in *Writers Express*.)

Writing Framework
Writers Express Student Handbook

The types of writing covered in the *Writers Express* handbook are listed below in a possible sequence, or framework, moving from personal forms to writing that becomes more and more public. The framework shows how the handbook can serve as students' primary writing resource for grades 4 and 5.

	Level 4	Level 5
PERSONAL WRITING		
Recording	Writing in Journals (105) Writing to Learn (243)	Writing in Journals (105) Writing to Learn (243)
Recalling and Remembering	Narrative Paragraph (63) Writing Personal Narratives (110)	Narrative Paragraph (63) A Writing Sampler (78)
SUBJECT WRITING		
Introducing	Sharing Family Stories (46)	Writing About a Special Person (79)
Describing	Descriptive Paragraph (62) Writing Observation Reports (148)	Descriptive Paragraph (62) Writing About a Special Object (82)
Reporting	Writing Newspaper Stories (123)	Writing Newspaper Stories (123)
Corresponding	Writing Friendly Letters (116) Writing a Letter of Request (143)	Writing Friendly Letters (116) Writing a Letter of Complaint (143)
Informing	Expository Paragraph (65) Writing Explanations (138)	Expository Paragraph (65) Writing Informational Essays (72)
Searching and Researching	Writing a Summary (216)	Writing a Summary (216) Writing a Classroom Report (220)
CREATIVE WRITING		
Imagining	Writing Tall Tales (160) Writing Realistic Stories (164)	Writing Fantasies (153) Writing Stories from History (170)
Inventing	Writing Free-Verse Poems (177) Invented Poetry (186) Writing Plays (192)	Writing Free-Verse Poems (177) Traditional Poetry (184) Writing Songs (188)
REFLECTIVE WRITING		
Applying and Analyzing	Applying Information (303) Comparing and Contrasting (297)	Cause and Effect Writing (304) Problems and Solutions (313)
Persuading	Persuasive Paragraph (64)	Writing a Letter to the Editor (131, 143)
Reviewing	Writing Book Reviews (132)	Writing a Review with a Special Focus (136)

The Process of Writing

The Writing Process (pages 6-7)

Open the handbook to pages 6 & 7 and have students follow the signs: prewriting, writing the first draft, revising, and editing & proofreading. Point out that these red, purple, orange, and green headings are used throughout *Writers Express*, wherever the four parts of the writing process are discussed. These colorful reminders reinforce this process in the numerous forms of writing addressed in the handbook, from classroom reports to poetry.

Exploring One Writer's Process (pages 8-11)

If students find it difficult to get a firm handle on using the writing process, suggest that they work along with Hillary—from prewriting to proofreading—in *One Writer's Process*.

A Basic Writing Guide (pages 12-15)

This guide addresses all aspects of writing. Students will find these valuable tips and reminders useful in science and history writing as well as in language arts class.

Planning Portfolios (pages 18-21)

Students may already save their best or favorite papers from previous school years. Invite them to expand their current system for keeping their written work by referring them to *Planning Your Portfolio*. The more students assume ownership of their writing, the more satisfaction they will experience, and the more time and effort they will invest in future writing projects.

Writing Ideas (pages 23-35)

Invite students to use the *Prewriting and Drafting Guide* to help them find "starting points" for doing assignments as well as writing for fun.

Reviewing, Revising, Rewriting (pages 37-41)

When it's time to rewrite, students are often unsure about what to delete and what to add, especially when they think the writing is already their best. After they complete a first draft, direct them to *Revising Your Writing*. Here they'll find revising advice, from how to "show," not "tell" to adding a good title.

Conferencing (pages 42-45, 322-327)

Writing can be a solitary process; but others can also be involved, from initial prewriting to final editing and proofreading. When students need or want others' help, use *Conferencing with Partners* and *Working in Groups*. These sections are especially useful for small-group work.

Models (pages 62-65, 79-83)

The sample paragraphs in *Writing Paragraphs* and the student essays in *A Writing Sampler* are just a few of the many forms of writing discussed and demonstrated through models in *Writers Express*. Samples are included for letters, book reviews, explanations, reports, plays, riddles, songs, poems, and more.

The Forms of Writing

Personal Writing (pages 105-121)

Personal writing is a lifelong skill. Throughout the year, ask students to try the five kinds of journal writing discussed in the handbook. Use *Writing Personal Narratives* to help students gain confidence for all their writing tasks, as they learn to share stories from their own lives. In addition, *Writing Friendly Letters* offers students a practical outlet for their personal writing. Encourage them to write invitations to other classes, thank-yous to field-trip chaperones, and class letters to parents.

Subject Writing (pages 123-151)

Writing Newspaper Stories helps students discover the kind of accountability called for in journalism. They will find another use for their reporting skills in *Writing Book Reviews*. Help students to sharpen their attention to detail and their ability to write careful description in *Writing Explanations* and *Writing Observation Reports*. Also refer students to *Writing Business Letters* when they find themselves in need of information or material for research projects.

Creative Writing (pages 153-205)

Whether students are seeking direction for their own creative writing, or working on literature-based activities, they'll enjoy the handbook's insights into fantasy and tall-tale writing. Students with a natural bent for nonfiction should be encouraged to investigate *Writing Realistic Stories* and *Writing Stories from History*, both popular genres for young people today.

Writing Poems offers students the tools needed to experiment with their language in poetry. *Writing Songs* offers a special twist on poetry writing. With their unique sensitivity and openness, students are natural playwrights. Use *Writing Plays* to create opportunities for drama in your classroom: skits, reenactments of scenes from current reading, reports, group presentations, and so on.

The creative writing section of *Writers Express* would not be complete without *Writing Riddles* and *Writing for Fun*, which emphasize the fun and enjoyment of playing with language. It's an important perspective for all learning situations.

Research Writing (pages 207-233)

Review *Using the Library* early in the school year. In addition to tips for finding information in encyclopedias and magazine guides, there is a list of other reference books and helpful guidelines for using them. This section also illustrates the use of card catalogs and computer searches. *Writing a Summary* would be a logical starting point for the kind of writing students might later do in *Writing a Classroom Report*.

The Tools of Learning

Building Vocabulary Skills (pages 255-273)

Review *Building Vocabulary Skills* to remind students of the many ways dictionaries and thesauruses can be useful in their writing. Encourage students to refer to the lists of prefixes, suffixes, and roots as they grapple with new words. Show them how easy it is to learn new words by becoming familiar with some of the most common word parts. In *Becoming a Better Speller,* students will discover strategies for spelling new words and for solving old spelling problems.

Reading and Viewing (pages 237-253, 288-291)

Whether students need to know how to watch a television special—*Improving Viewing Skills*—or read charts and graphs—*Reading Pictures*—or improve their study- reading skills—*Using Reading Strategies*—they'll find helpful suggestions in these sections of the handbook.

Giving Speeches (pages 275-281)

If students are doing impromptu speeches, or presenting formal classroom reports, direct them to *Giving Speeches.* This chapter presents writing a speech (or preparing any oral presentation) from start to delivery. The five performance tips in *Performing Poems* can also apply to individual or group presentations.

Improving Your Thinking (pages 295-313)

Students must learn to organize their time, their efforts, and their materials. These skills apply equally to math, science, and history. In *Getting Organized*, students will find graphic organizers to help coordinate material and a "thinking moves" chart to help direct their thinking. Students are often asked to write in ways that show their abilities to recall, understand, apply, analyze, synthesize, or evaluate information. To better understand and use these ways of writing and thinking, students should study *Thinking and Writing.* When they need to know the difference between fact and opinion, how to avoid fuzzy thinking, how to make a decision, or how to solve a problem, they can turn to *Thinking Clearly.*

Improving Your Learning Skills (pages 315-339)

Students learn how to plan, listen, cooperate, and make decisions together in the chapter about working in groups. Refer students to *Keeping Good Notes* and *Taking Tests* to help them use their writing skills for effective learning.

The Proofreader's Guide

Check It Out! (pages 343-387)

For spot-checking grammar, punctuation, mechanics, usage, and commonly misspelled words, students will refer to the *Proofreader's Guide* again and again. The yellow pages make this handy reference section easy to find, while the examples and color codes make the material easy to understand.

The Student Almanac

Tables, Lists, Maps, Time Line (pages 391-439)

Point out the helpful and interesting reference information in *The Student Almanac.* The tables and lists cover sign language, foreign words, animal facts, the metric system, conversion tables, additional units of measure, planet profiles, an index to world maps, topographic information, common and advanced math symbols, prime numbers, basic multiplication facts, decimal equivalents of common fractions, roman numerals, the computer keyboard and fingering chart, articles of the Constitution, amendments to the Constitution, U.S. presidents and vice presidents, and the order of presidential succession.

Using Maps not only offers 10 full-color maps of the world, but also discusses map symbols, legends, map scales, longitude and latitude, coordinates, and how to use all this information.

Improving Math Skills walks students through basic problem-solving thinking and demonstrates the process through sample problems.

The U.S. Constitution is discussed in *History in the Making.* There's also a time line covering U.S. history, science and inventions, and literature and life from 1492 to the present—including significant contributions, discoveries, and events from around the world.

The Process of Writing

"The Process of Writing" section in *Writers Express* contains everything your students need to know about writing—from a basic look at the steps in the writing process to a comprehensive list of interesting writing forms, from guidelines for writing paragraphs and essays to guidelines for combining sentences. Once your students become familiar with all of this information, they will turn to this section again and again, whenever they have a question about their writing. The table of contents below lists all of the chapters in "The Process of Writing" section of the handbook. The page numbers refer to the location of each chapter summary in this guide.

Special Note: For minilessons related to the writing process, see pages 93-97.

Getting Started

All About Writing

(pages 3-7)

Introduction

This chapter introduces students to the writing process as well as to the idea of writing to learn. Students are assured that they can understand and use this process of writing, which will result in better thinking and learning.

All About Writing begins by telling the "real" story about writing—that writing is natural, that it is useful, that much of it involves a time commitment, and that it requires practice. The complete writing process is spelled out for students, with an important reminder that the steps are not always sequential.

Rationale

- ***Through writing, students can discover a lot about how they think and learn.***
- ***The writing process lets students experience how writers really work.***
- ***Students who succeed in getting their thoughts down in writing feel better able to cope with writing assignments and tests that require writing.***

Major Concepts

- ☐ **Writing to learn is a very natural process.** (page 4)
- ☐ **Writing allows students to think on paper, a useful, lifelong skill.** (page 4)
- ☐ **Learning to write involves understanding that writing is a process that is not always sequential or linear.** (page 5)
- ☐ **Writing for others often involves prewriting, drafting, revising, editing, proofreading, and publishing.** (pages 5-7)

One Writer's Process

(pages 8-11)

Introduction

Donald Murray has described writing as "a process of continuous thinking, experimenting, and reviewing." While the activity of writing can be described in stages (prewriting, drafting, revising, and editing/proofreading), we remember Murray's point—within any stage, writers think, experiment, and review. We revise our thoughts as we prewrite; we rewrite as we draft; we experiment with lines as we revise; and so on.

In ***One Writer's Process***, students observe Hillary Bachman at work on "A Great Teacher." Students see her collect her thoughts, attempt a draft, work with a friend while revising, and edit and proofread for clarity and correctness.

Rationale

- ***Because many students don't know that all writers struggle, it is important to show them a student-writer at work.***
- ***Devoting attention to generating ideas, planning writing, drafting with an experimental attitude, and being prepared to rewrite are worthy goals for all students.***
- ***Students need to understand that collaboration with a peer can often help them achieve clarity.***

Major Concepts

- ☐ **Prewriting involves selecting a subject and collecting details.** (page 8)
- ☐ **First drafts are often written freely.** (page 9)
- ☐ **When revising, writers look at overall completeness and clarity.** (page 10)
- ☐ **When editing and proofreading, writers look at every word.** (page 11)

A Basic Writing Guide

(pages 12-15)

Introduction

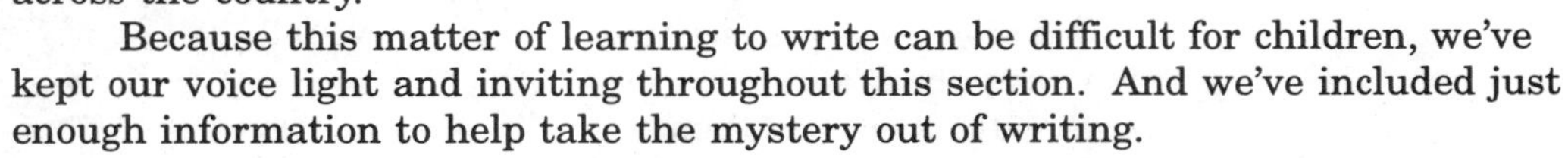

Children are filled with questions and worries about their learning, just as teachers are about their teaching. So in this chapter, ***A Basic Writing Guide,*** we answer the writing questions we get most often from children across the country.

Because this matter of learning to write can be difficult for children, we've kept our voice light and inviting throughout this section. And we've included just enough information to help take the mystery out of writing.

Rationale

- ***Students need to know that their teachers understand they have gnawing questions about writing. This chapter lays several on the line.***
- ***The answers to these common questions are straightforward, letting students know that writing need not be mysterious.***

Major Concepts

- ☐ **It helps to write about topics of high personal interest.** (page 12)
- ☐ **The amount of prewriting a student does depends on his or her topic.** (page 13)
- ☐ **Writing involves selecting what to put in a draft.** (page 13)
- ☐ **First-draft writing requires a free spirit.** (page 14)
- ☐ **Students and their friends can often judge what changes need to be made.** (page 14)
- ☐ **Students should be expected to make as many grammar, mechanics, and usage corrections as they can.** (page 15)
- ☐ **If students write about topics of high interest, attempt to write in an interesting way, and work at correcting their errors, they should allow themselves to feel good about their writing.** (page 15)

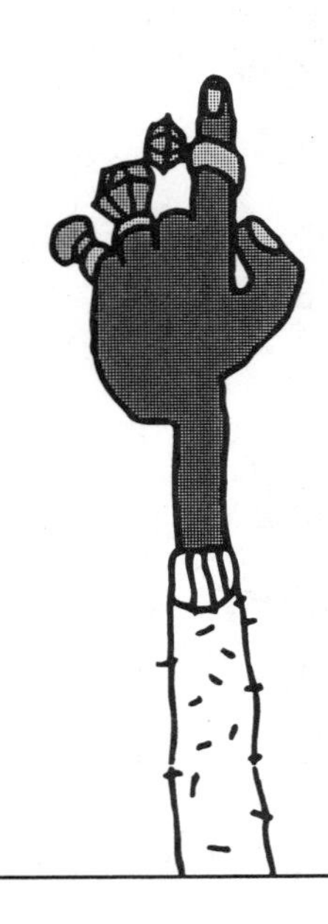

Writing with a Computer

(pages 16-17)

Introduction

As we all know, technology is becoming more available—and more appropriate—for students to use, especially in the area of writing. But, for many of us, using technology in our classrooms means restructuring. Those of us who didn't grow up writing with computers, and those of us who still don't use them much, may be a little skeptical. That's only natural. It helps to remember what Marilyn Ferguson said about change: "It is not so much that we're afraid of change, or so in love with the old ways, but it's that place in between . . . it's like being in between trapezes. It's Linus when his blanket is in the dryer. There's nothing to hold on to."

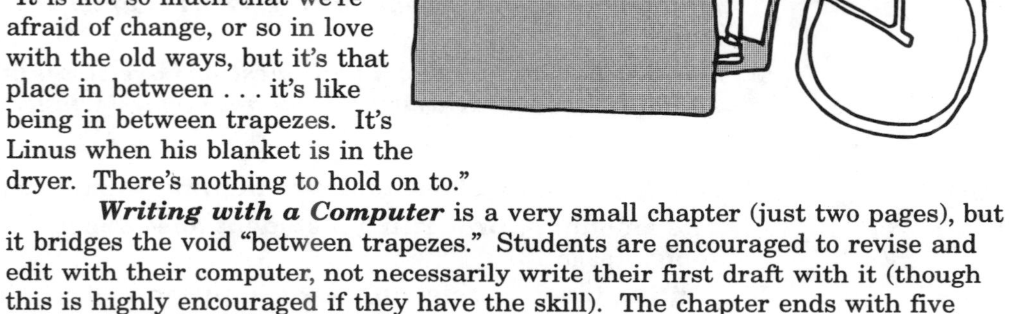

Writing with a Computer is a very small chapter (just two pages), but it bridges the void "between trapezes." Students are encouraged to revise and edit with their computer, not necessarily write their first draft with it (though this is highly encouraged if they have the skill). The chapter ends with five helpful comments about computers and writing.

Rationale

- ***Computers are a part of modern life that students should know about.***
- ***Educators are finding ways to use computers to enhance learning.***
- ***Computer labs, on-line computer services, and various other technologies are common throughout the country.***

Major Concepts

- ☐ **Many writers use personal computers.** (page 16)
- ☐ **It's important to be able to sort out how and when to count on a machine.** (page 17)

Planning Your Portfolio

(pages 18-21)

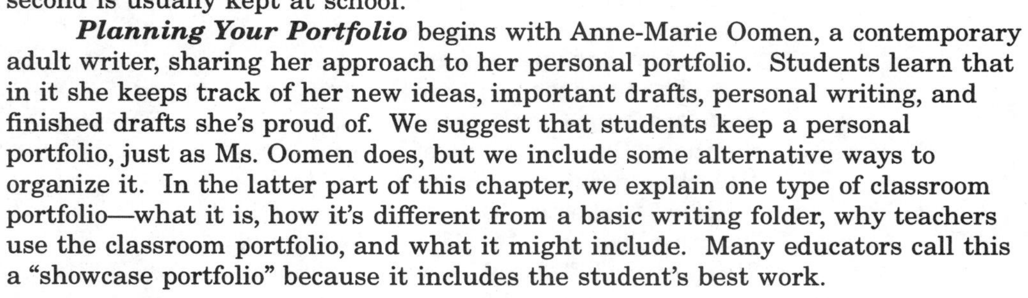

Introduction

Two types of portfolios are mentioned in *Writers Express:* personal writing portfolios and classroom writing portfolios. Both are collections of work—the first is usually kept at home, the second is usually kept at school.

Planning Your Portfolio begins with Anne-Marie Oomen, a contemporary adult writer, sharing her approach to her personal portfolio. Students learn that in it she keeps track of her new ideas, important drafts, personal writing, and finished drafts she's proud of. We suggest that students keep a personal portfolio, just as Ms. Oomen does, but we include some alternative ways to organize it. In the latter part of this chapter, we explain one type of classroom portfolio—what it is, how it's different from a basic writing folder, why teachers use the classroom portfolio, and what it might include. Many educators call this a "showcase portfolio" because it includes the student's best work.

Rationale

- ***When students keep portfolios, they are taking charge of their own learning by reflecting on their work and their learning processes.***
- ***Standardized tests cannot effectively measure all learning and teaching, so portfolios offer another assessment perspective.***
- ***Portfolios require student reflection and choice. If properly supported, self-assessment, rather than outside forces, can drive personal learning.***

Major Concepts

- ☐ **Each writer's personal portfolio says something about his or her talent and writing process.** (page 18)
- ☐ **A personal portfolio might include writing ideas, current drafts, "personal" writing, and finished work.** (page 19)
- ☐ **A classroom portfolio is often a collection of each student's best work.** (page 20)
- ☐ **The work included in a classroom portfolio might have a due date.** (page 21)

Prewriting & Drafting Guide

(pages 23-35)

Introduction and Rationale

All of us know that explosions of thought occur as we write. It is just as true, however, that most writers carefully plan their time, keep lists of ideas, clip excerpts of great writing for reference, and so on. In other words, writers engage in many behind-the-scenes activities to support their writing. It is an exciting process—one that is interactive, ongoing, and enriching.

The handbook section ***Prewriting and Drafting Guide*** contains six chapters: "Building a File of Writing Ideas," "Selecting a Subject," "Starting Points for Writing," "Collecting Details," "Planning and Drafting Tips," and "Building a Resource of Writing Forms." Think of them as buoys supporting your students' ongoing writing activity. These chapters will help your students when they need a writing idea, need to collect details, or need planning or drafting help.

Major Concepts

- ☐ **Ideas for writing surround us.** (pages 24-25)
- ☐ **Using strategies for discovering subjects makes prewriting easier.** (pages 26-27)
- ☐ **At times, prompts, quotations, and general topics can help students discover writing subjects.** (pages 28-29)
- ☐ **There are three basic ways to collect facts and details about a subject.** (pages 30-31)
- ☐ **Plans keep writers organized; a good attitude keeps writers writing.** (pages 32-33)
- ☐ **Knowing about different forms of writing helps writers write.** (pages 34-35)

Revising Your Writing

(pages 37-41)

Introduction

Writers improve upon what they have written by rereading their writing and rewriting the parts that need work. This process is called *revision*. Among other things, writers read and listen for meaning, authority, voice, and clarity. Careful writers also listen for fully developed, connected thinking as they revise.

On the first page of ***Revising Your Writing,*** a quote by young writer Lauren Brydon reminds fellow students that writing takes time and energy. The remaining words on this page mirror Lauren's sentiments, and the chapter continues by defining revision and suggesting how to get started and how to progress. A revising checklist is provided, followed by a collection of revision tips. The chapter ends with a reminder: "Take Note: You may have to revise your writing two or three times before all of your ideas are clear and complete."

Rationale

■ ***Many students think that good writers sit down and write finished, polished pieces the first time through. This rarely happens.***

■ ***Many students worry about revision because they feel their ideas will be changed. Information about the revision process can lead to new and healthier understandings.***

■ ***Time away from a draft helps writers see how close they've come to saying what they mean and gives them a chance to say it better.***

Major Concepts

☐ **Writing can be changed before it's published—unlike real-life conversation—so that it more closely reflects what you mean.** (page 37)

☐ **The revision process becomes more efficient when writers take a break from their writing.** (page 38)

☐ **Revision is easier when writers have the benefit of another pair of eyes.** (page 38)

☐ **Writers can *show* rather than *tell* their readers what they mean by using the five senses.** (page 40)

☐ **Writers need to check that they've included enough details to give their writing clarity and authority.** (page 41)

☐ **Writers should be sure their piece is complete, having a beginning, a middle, and an ending.** (page 41)

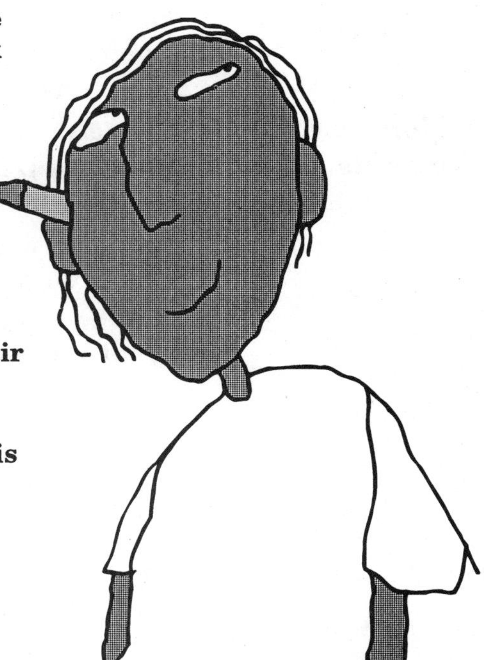

Conferencing with Partners

(pages 42-45)

Introduction

When students talk about their writing to others, they are holding a conference. The process of conferring with partners gives student writers insight, which in turn helps them gain control over their writing process.

Conferencing with Partners begins by discussing the writer's need to read evolving drafts to others. The handbook reminds students that whenever they ask for an ear, and they do quite often, they are acting like real writers. Next, author and listener guidelines are laid out to show students how to make the most of their time by coming to conferences prepared. The chapter ends with two types of response sheets, which encourage listeners to write their thoughts down as they talk to authors. This way authors can refer to these notes later as they revise.

Rationale

- ***As writers review their writing, they try to look at it with "new eyes." It follows that another approach is to literally bring in others' eyes.***
- ***Almost any friendly response helps sustain children's interest in their writing.***
- ***When writers read their work to others and get a response, it can be a great breakthrough. They realize their hard work affects others.***
- ***When conferring is part of a writing program, students learn how to talk about writing and how to receive and use information from others.***

Major Concepts

- ☐ **Conferencing with partners can help students revise.** (page 43)
- ☐ **Students learn that the feedback they receive, in the form of observations, lets them know how their drafts affect others.** (page 44)
- ☐ **By using conference guidelines, writers learn what is powerful, what is useful, and what is well understood in their work.** (page 44)
- ☐ **Writing down responses is a good way to help students remember what was said during a conference.** (page 45)

Sharing Family Stories

(pages 46-49)

Introduction

By writing family stories, students will come to feel the strength and knowledge that is deeply rooted in human families. Marie Ponsot and Rosemary Deen, major contributors to this chapter, call these family stories "parables"—stories that illustrate family life and the lessons we learn from it. They are simple stories, often told over and over again by family members.

Sharing Family Stories has been carefully designed so that students can learn to write a family story from direct experience, just by following the directions in the handbook. A short student model is provided, as are step-by-step instructions. In addition to introducing the parable form, the actions called for throughout this unit (reading, listening, rereading, and writing) lead students to talk with and listen to one another—important parts of learning to write well.

Rationale

- ***Students can write about their families from direct experience.***
- ***Students listen actively because each new parable they read or listen to naturally interests them. They can relate to stories about brothers, sisters, friends, and relatives.***
- ***Sharing stories and making descriptive observations about them takes students beyond the "I like it" or "I don't like it" responses.***
- ***Students are given opportunities to inductively learn the inner logic of the parable form through the process of writing, reading, and listening.***
- ***This chapter requires undistracted rereading, which is indispensable to rewriting.***

Major Concepts

- ☐ **Family parables are stories that we hear and tell over and over again.** (pages 46-47)
- ☐ **Choosing a topic results naturally from thinking about many possible stories.** (page 48)
- ☐ **A good family parable can be any length.** (page 48)
- ☐ **Students are encouraged to make written observations that describe what interests them about a shared story.** (page 49)

Planning Notes

MATERIALS NEEDED: Gather examples of family stories from your school library.

READING/WRITING CONNECTIONS: Encourage your students to include one or two of their stories in letters to family members and friends. Have them ask these people to write back with family stories of their own.

ACROSS-THE-CURRICULUM POSSIBILITIES: Biographies and historical fiction are filled with family stories that have shaped human experience. These stories can be read in conjunction with social studies and science units. Look for these throughout the year, and make a habit of pointing them out to your students.

Editing and Proofreading

(pages 50-53)

Introduction

Up to this point, students have been working at making their writing complete and creative. The ideas are clear now. The important points have been made. When they read the piece aloud, partners say, "Cool. I get it now." But wait! There's one more step in the process before publishing. The writing must be edited and proofread. More specifically, the inevitable bumps in sentence structure need to be smoothed out, and the nasty errors in mechanics and usage must be eliminated.

Editing and Proofreading offers clear guidelines for polishing writing. Tips on combining short sentences, changing monotonous sentence beginnings, and correcting errors like fragments and run-ons should prove useful. Guidelines for choosing powerful verbs, specific nouns, and colorful modifiers and for avoiding usage errors are also provided. Finally, a handy checklist restates these points, adding reminders (and handbook references) about correct punctuation, capitalization, and spelling.

Rationale

- ***Published (shared) writing that contains errors (mechanical/ structural/ word choice) may not be taken seriously.***
- ***Students who have worked to write and revise their thoughts deserve to know how to edit and proofread their writing.***
- ***Students can take pride in a neat, correct final draft of their work.***

Major Concepts

- ☐ **Editing and proofreading means polishing your writing—getting rid of careless errors and making every word count.** (page 50)
- ☐ **One of the main editing tasks is making sentences read smoothly. This is done by combining, working on sentence beginnings, and correcting structural errors (fragments, run-ons, rambling).** (page 51)
- ☐ **Another important editing task is choosing the right words. This involves using powerful words and avoiding usage errors.** (page 52)
- ☐ **An editing and proofreading checklist is an invaluable tool that contains important reminders about proper punctuation, capitalization, and spelling.** (page 53)

Publishing Your Writing

(pages 54-57)

Introduction

It's really something when a fourth-grade boy's single most significant memory of the year is his teacher "publishing" his Thanksgiving turkey on the chalkboard and commenting to the class on how good it is. Kent Brown is that fourth-grade boy, and today he's the publisher of *Highlights for Children*, the most widely read children's magazine in the world. Kent Brown would say publishing is powerful stuff: He doesn't remember even one classmate's name, but the memory of his teacher publishing his turkey has stuck with him for almost a half century. This story appears as the foreword to a book by Kathy Henderson, *The Market Guide for Young Writers,* devoted solely to the topic of publishing children's work.

Publishing Your Writing begins by suggesting many ways to publish students' work. They can mail it, perform it, print it, or submit it. Addresses are provided for submission purposes, and a final segment shows one way to bind books for classroom publication.

Rationale

- ***When work is published, it suggests it is worthy of publication. Seeing one's own work published helps build self-esteem.***
- ***By reading other students' work (fiction and nonfiction), young people discover how others in their class solve dilemmas, fantasize, dream, and understand their world.***
- ***Published writers want to write more, and they tend to read more. Readers who write, read like writers—such readers do so with an eye and ear for voice, style, structure, details, flow, and language.***

Major Concepts

- ☐ **Publishing makes writing worth the effort.** (page 54)
- ☐ **Ways to publish span all the language arts.** (pages 54-57)
- ☐ **Books can be bound at home.** (page 57)

Writing Paragraphs

(pages 59-71)

Introduction

A paragraph focuses on one specific topic developed as a story, a description, an explanation, or an opinion. The form depends upon the topic, the kinds of details the writer is able to gather, and the audience. Whatever form the paragraph takes, it must contain enough supporting detail to give the reader a complete and interesting picture of the topic.

Writing Paragraphs begins by defining a paragraph and explaining its basic parts. Student models illustrate the four types of paragraphs, and a step-by-step plan for writing a paragraph follows. Next the handbook explains where and how to gather information as well as three methods for putting the details in good order. A comprehensive chart of transition or linking words follows. The chapter ends by explaining a three-step process for finding paragraphs in writing that lacks appropriate paragraph breaks.

Rationale

- ***Real-world writing (news releases, directions to a specific place, short introductions, simple explanations, etc.) often involves the construction of simple paragraphs.***
- ***Paragraphs are the conceptual building blocks for stories, essays, and articles. Writing them gives children the opportunity to think conceptually.***
- ***Sentences within paragraphs and paragraphs within longer texts require linking and transition words. Learning how to use these words effectively is an important writing and thinking skill.***
- ***Paragraphs help readers make sense of longer pieces of writing; therefore, learning how to find paragraphs in one's own writing is crucial to effective communication.***

Major Concepts

- ☐ **A paragraph is a group of sentences that tells about one subject or idea.** (page 59)
- ☐ **Paragraphs have three basic parts: the topic sentence, the body, and the closing sentence.** (pages 60-61)
- ☐ **There are different types of paragraphs.** (pages 62-65)
- ☐ **Planning is an important step in the process of writing paragraphs.** (page 66)
- ☐ **The details used in paragraphs come from various sources.** (page 67)
- ☐ **Paragraphs can be organized in different ways.** (page 68)
- ☐ **Transition or linking words glue sentences in paragraphs together and help readers understand sentence-level relationships.** (page 69)

Writing Essays

(pages 72-77)

Introduction

The process of writing essays is really thinking on paper—thinking to make connections, form understandings, raise questions, and find answers. No other form of writing, in fact, gets students so thoughtfully involved in their learning. In this respect, it is never too early to have students write essays, especially essays that stem from their own interests and concerns.

The opening page in ***Writing Essays*** addresses two important points: It assures students that they are "thinking" essays all the time, and it identifies the basic characteristics of this form of writing. The next page discusses three fundamental reasons to write essays: to present information, to share a strong opinion, and to make everyone think. Then, in the pages that follow, students are provided with step-by-step writing guidelines, a model essay, and tips for organizing supporting facts and details.

Rationale

- ***Writing essays helps students organize their thoughts and feelings about factual information.***
- ***Learning the essay-writing process prepares students for the different expository writing tasks they will be asked to carry out.***
- ***Sharing essays opens up discussions on important and timely subjects.***

Major Concepts

- ☐ **There are three basic reasons to write essays: to present information, to share a strong opinion, and to make everyone think.** (page 73)
- ☐ **To begin planning an essay, a writer should select an interesting subject and identify his or her audience.** (page 74)
- ☐ **As a writer continues planning, he or she should decide upon a special part of the subject (or a focus) to develop.** (page 74)
- ☐ **Each part of an essay—the beginning, the middle, and the ending—plays a special role.** (page 75)
- ☐ **Listing, clustering/webbing, and outlining can help writers organize the facts and details in their essays.** (page 77)

Planning Notes

READING/WRITING CONNECTIONS: Have your students read and react to essays in current magazines for young readers (*Weekly Reader, Sports Illustrated for Kids,* etc.). Refer to these essays when you discuss different parts of the handbook chapter.

ACROSS-THE-CURRICULUM POSSIBILITIES: Essay writing should be encouraged in all areas of the curriculum. For example, in social studies, students could express (and support) their opinions about important current events. In art or music, they could present information about someone or something they have recently learned about. In science, they could present a thoughtful analysis of an environmental issue, and so on.

A Writing Sampler

(pages 78-83)

Introduction

In *The Writer in All of Us,* writer and teacher June Gould praises the power of writing personal stories. She states, "Telling your story certifies that you are who you are—that you belong—that you have a special place in the scheme of things." We, too, praise the power of writing about personal experiences, and we want young writers to feel this power as well. That is why we developed this "sampler" of personal stories and essays. After your students read and enjoy these models, they should be primed to tell their own stories, to "certify" that they have something special to say about the people, places, and events in their lives.

The opening page of ***A Writing Sampler*** encourages students to write about their personal experiences. Each page that follows addresses a different type of personal writing: writing about a person, a place, an event, an object, and a condition. Brief introductory remarks, concise prewriting guidelines, and an annotated student model are provided for each type of writing. That is more than enough to get students started on their own personal stories.

Rationale

- ***Students need to learn to write from within, drawing inspiration and ideas from all the different people, places, and events in their past experiences.***
- ***It's important that students understand that writing is a powerful learning tool.***
- ***Students need to appreciate the value of models when it comes to developing their own writing.***

Major Concepts

- ☐ **All students have special people, places, events, and objects to write about.** (page 78)
- ☐ **Writing about personal experiences develops a writer's storytelling skills.** (page 78)
- ☐ **People, places, events, and objects in a writer's life are good sources for writing ideas.** (pages 78-83)
- ☐ **Prewriting involves selecting an effective subject and collecting details.** (pages 79-83)
- ☐ **When developing a piece of writing, it's important to think in terms of the beginning, middle, and ending.** (pages 79-83)

Planning Notes

READING/WRITING CONNECTION: Collect personal stories from magazines, newspapers, nonfiction books, and anthologies for your students to read during their work in this chapter. Also encourage students to collect personal stories on their own to share with their classmates.

Writing Basic Sentences

(pages 85-89)

Introduction

When students are ready to edit their writing, one of the first things they should do is review the sentences in their work. Each sentence should express a clear and complete thought and effectively fit in with the rest of the writing. You can use this chapter to review sentences with your students at the beginning of the year; they, in turn, can refer to it whenever they have a question about the sentences in their writing.

On the introductory page of ***Writing Basic Sentences***, the importance of using complete sentences is discussed. Next, a review of the basic parts of a sentence is provided. The following pages address sentence errors (fragments, run-on sentences, etc.), subject-verb agreement, and special sentence problems (double subjects, double negatives, etc.).

Rationale

- ***It's important for students to fine-tune their sentence sense, to know what is and what isn't a sentence.***
- ***Students need to know what to look for when they edit the sentences in their writing.***
- ***Students need to take pride in their writing and strive to express their ideas clearly and effectively.***

Major Concepts

- ☐ **Checking for sentence errors is an important editing task.** (page 85)
- ☐ **All sentences have two basic parts—the subject and the verb.** (page 86)
- ☐ **Common sentence errors include sentence fragments, run-on sentences, and rambling sentences.** (page 87)
- ☐ **The subjects and verbs in sentences must agree.** (page 88)
- ☐ **Sentences should be checked for double subjects, pronoun/antecedent agreement problems, double negatives, and so on.** (page 89)

Planning Notes

HANDBOOK CONSIDERATION: For a detailed review of sentences—including discussions of the parts, types, and kinds of sentences—refer to "Understanding Sentences" on pages 370-373 in the handbook.

Combining Sentences

(pages 90-93)

Introduction

Study after study has sung the praises of sentence combining. No other specific activity, in fact, has been shown to do so much to improve writing quality, especially in terms of syntactic proficiency. Sentence-combining practice is important for all student writers, regardless of their grade levels (from second grade on up) or their ability levels. The ability to combine sentences becomes most helpful during revising and editing, when sentence structure becomes the focus of a writer's attention.

Combining Sentences discusses three basic types of sentence combining: combining with a key word or series of words, combining with phrases, and combining with longer sentences. Easy-to-follow explanations and examples are provided for each type of combining.

Rationale

- ***Sentence combining promotes greater skill in writing sentences.***
- ***Sentence combining helps students become more attentive to their writing.***
- ***Sentence combining also helps students become more appreciative of the language.***

Major Concepts

- ☐ **Ideas from short sentences can be combined by moving a key word from one sentence to the other.** (page 91)
- ☐ **Ideas from short sentences can be combined into one sentence using a series of key words or phrases.** (page 91)
- ☐ **Ideas from short sentences can be combined into one sentence using a phrase.** (page 92)
- ☐ **Two sentences can be combined using compound subjects or verbs.** (page 92)
- ☐ **Two or more simple sentences can be combined into a compound sentence.** (page 93)
- ☐ **Two or more ideas can be combined in a complex sentence.** (page 93)

Planning Notes

HANDBOOK CONSIDERATION: Refer to "Understanding Sentences" on pages 370-373 in the handbook for more information related to the challenging concepts of phrases, compound sentences, and complex sentences covered in this chapter.

Modeling the Masters

(pages 96-97)

Introduction

Just as beginning artists learn about art by studying the works of famous painters, young writers can learn about writing by studying the works of good authors. The process of emulating the writing patterns and styles of professional writers is often referred to as modeling.

Modeling the Masters provides five guidelines that will help your students increase their use of words and improve their ability to craft sentences. Two examples of professional writing and a student's modeling attempts are provided.

Rationale

- ***As they study the works of their favorite authors and learn new ways to use words and compose sentences, students become more flexible writers.***
- ***Artists often model the work they admire and then slowly incorporate what they like into their own works.***

Major Concepts

- ☐ **Students' writing skills can be enhanced through the careful study of sentences and short passages from the books and other writings of favorite authors.** (pages 96-97)
- ☐ **Modeling an author's pattern of writing will help students create new patterns for their own writing.** (page 97)

Planning Notes

RELATED MATERIALS: Students can select their favorite authors to model after reading through this short unit. Anthologies and works of popular authors should be available in the classroom.

READING/WRITING CONNECTIONS: The handbook chapter focuses on modeling a master's writing style, but students may also want to model how writers work. Sixteen poets talk to students about all sorts of patterns, including how they write, in the book *Speaking of Poets: Interview with Poets Who Write for Children and Young Adults* by Jeffrey S. Copland (National Council of Teachers of English, 1993). Young authors can also see how writers find ideas in Sandy Asher's paperback *Where Do You Get Your Ideas? Helping Young Writers Begin* (Walker and Company, 1993). Furthermore, students will be interested in how authors their age work as they read young-author interviews in *The Market Guide for Young Writers: Where and How to Sell What You Write* by Kathy Henderson (Writer's Digest, 1993).

ACROSS-THE-CURRICULUM POSSIBILITIES: Writers, scholars, and inventors all stand on the shoulders of others. Your students might begin to understand the power of modeling/mentoring/being-influenced-by as they read over the handbook's time line (pages 430-439). Have them look for a favorite person in any discipline; then ask them to do some research, digging specifically for the mention of mentors or influences. Your class might draw a sort of family tree (see handbook page 248), relating one historical figure to another. It will become apparent that those who aspire to do something well, look to others for knowledge and inspiration.

The Forms of Writing

You can build a timely and comprehensive writing program around "The Forms of Writing" section in *Writers Express*. Included in this section of the handbook are guidelines for writing personal narratives, book reviews, business letters, tall tales, poems, plays, and much more. The table of contents below lists all of the chapters in "The Forms of Writing" section of the handbook. The page numbers refer to the location of each chapter summary in this guide.

Special Note: For minilessons related to the forms of writing, see pages 98-102.

Personal Writing

Subject Writing

Writing Tales and Stories

Writing Poems, Plays, and Stories

Research Writing

Writing in Journals

(pages 105-109)

Introduction

A journal can be a notebook with blank pages or a simple, stapled stack of paper. In journals, students write to learn by making observations, capturing memories, and responding to literature and by questioning, analyzing, synthesizing, and reflecting upon their school learning and other life experiences.

Writing in Journals begins with an invitation to use journal writing as a way to handle a terrible day. Then several reasons are listed for writing in a personal journal, and guidelines are given to help students get started. Next students take a closer look at ways in which journal writing can prove powerful. The handbook urges students to reflect through questioning and wondering and to push themselves by reviewing old entries and making new connections.

Rationale

- ***Students learn by writing as they reflect on and process what they know and as they discover what they need to find out.***
- ***As students write regularly in journals, their writing becomes more fluent, a skill that will benefit them in all their writing tasks.***
- ***When seeking topics for writing, students can draw from their journal-recorded personal experiences.***

Major Concepts

- ☐ **Journal writing can be a daily activity.** (page 106)
- ☐ **There are ways to get started using journals and ways to keep going.** (page 106)
- ☐ **Journal writing involves different types of thinking.** (page 107)
- ☐ **Journal writing works best if students use it to reflect and to make new connections.** (page 107)
- ☐ **There are many different kinds of journals.** (pages 108-109)

Writing Personal Narratives

(pages 110-115)

Introduction

The best stories come from our most important memories, those that are significant and usually attached to a strong emotion. For students, thinking back on experiences and recalling details may not always be easy, but the work pays off in the form of a good story, a thoughtful retelling of things past.

Writing Personal Narratives begins with an explanation of personal narratives and how students can begin searching for possible subjects. Sandy Asher, the major contributor to this chapter, then shares a true story about herself and her family, "The Great Gerbil Escape," which is followed by guidelines for gathering ideas and writing a personal narrative. Students are given a few good revision tips about adding details, using the senses, using dialogue, and sharing thoughts and feelings. Finally, the chapter provides a student model, "When I Got Burned on My Dad's Motorcycle," complete with side notes.

Rationale

- ***Writing personal narratives puts students in touch with themselves and with the world in which they live.***
- ***Personal-narrative writing, with its ready supply of subject matter, is often an excellent starting point for reluctant writers.***

Major Concepts

- ☐ **A personal narrative is a story about a personal memory.** (page 110)
- ☐ **Students can gather ideas by writing in a daily diary or journal.** (page 112)
- ☐ **Students can follow specific steps in order to produce a satisfactory personal narrative.** (page 113)
- ☐ **Students can learn to enrich their stories with details, dialogue, and personal feelings.** (page 114)

Planning Notes

MATERIALS NEEDED: Have plenty of personal-narrative examples available in the classroom. Magazines such as *Highlights*, *Stone Soup*, *Cricket Magazine,* and *Cobblestone* often include personal narratives.

READING/WRITING CONNECTIONS: Some realistic fiction or books based on authors' lives would be excellent additions to the classroom library at this time. Consider *The Best Town in the World* by Byrd Baylor, *Nana Upstairs and Nana Downstairs* by Tomie dePaola, *The Relatives Came* and *When I Was Young in the Mountains* by Cynthia Rylant.

ACROSS-THE-CURRICULUM POSSIBILITIES: Students' personal narratives often include members of their extended families. These narratives could lead to the creation of family trees (handbook page 248), a life map (handbook page 25), or a time line (handbook pages 430-439).

Writing Friendly Letters

(pages 116-121)

Introduction

Everyone enjoys receiving personal mail, especially letters. Think of how quickly you flip through the mail each day, passing over envelopes marked "Occupant," grumbling internally about bills, all the while searching for something personal, just for you. This is the joy of receiving friendly letters, and it is felt by children and adults alike. Letters have the power to make friendships stronger and draw family members closer together. And as this chapter states, the best way to make sure that you receive a letter is to send one!

Writing Friendly Letters begins with an introduction to and a description of the parts of a friendly letter. Then a student model is presented, followed by steps and guidelines for writing friendly letters. The final section discusses two types of social notes, invitations and thank-you notes. Each are defined and models are provided.

Rationale

- ***Writing a friendly letter gives children the opportunity to express themselves freely about anything at all.***
- ***Receiving letters encourages students to write.***
- ***Learning how to communicate in writing is an important social skill.***

Major Concepts

- ☐ **A friendly letter has a heading, salutation, body, closing, and signature.** (pages 116-117)
- ☐ **There is a special method for addressing an envelope.** (page 119)
- ☐ **Invitations and thank-you notes have a salutation, body, closing, and signature.** (page 120)

Planning Notes

MATERIALS NEEDED: You may want to have a supply of appealing stationery, colored pens, rubber stamps, and ink pads for your students to use.

READING/WRITING CONNECTIONS: *The Jolly Postman and Other People's Letters* (by Janet and Allan Ahlberg, 1986) is a fun model for creative letter writing. The postman in this book delivers letters to fairy-tale characters. Reading these letters may prompt your students to write creative letters to their favorite fictional characters.

ACROSS-THE-CURRICULUM POSSIBILITIES: As your students study real people in science and social studies, use friendly letter writing as a report strategy. Let your students create a series of letters that these individuals might have received or sent at different points in their lives.

Writing Newspaper Stories

(pages 123-131)

Introduction

Roy Peter Clark, the principal contributor to this chapter, says, "Journalists see writing as a *transaction* between the writer and the reader." The writer makes choices about what to write, gathers information, decides what information to highlight, and tries to present readers with a clear and accurate finished story. The readers must interpret what's been said, knowing journalists make choices, and highlight what seems important to them. Reporting is quite a responsibility.

Writing Newspaper Stories zeros in on three forms: **news stories, human interest stories**, and **letters to the editor**. News and human interest stories are true accounts of events in the life of a community. They differ in that the human interest story doesn't necessarily deal with a timely and important happening. The letter to the editor is obviously an important form and serves as a natural introduction to persuasive writing.

Rationale

- ***Writing news stories feels important to young writers because there's an assumption that the writing will be published.***
- ***Many of the qualities we attribute to good writing—focus, coherence, design, and clarity—can be stressed while news stories are being written.***

Major Concepts

- ☐ **Interviewing is fundamental to newswriting.** (page 125)
- ☐ **Basic news stories need a limited focus and coherent structure.** (page 128)
- ☐ **News and human interest stories require good leads.** (page 130)
- ☐ **Writing a letter to the editor is one of the most important ways to practice freedom of expression and freedom of the press.** (page 131)

Planning Notes

RELATED MATERIALS: Roy Peter Clark highly recommends that children use small notebooks for their journalistic work. He feels small notebooks build confidence in a writer because filling up the pages creates a sense of momentum. Also have daily and student newspapers on hand.

READING/WRITING CONNECTIONS: One of the best ways to understand news stories is to read the local paper. Almost every daily paper offers school rates for limited periods of time. Also ask your students to search out small newsletters throughout their community.

PLANNING YOUR OWN CLASSROOM NEWSPAPER: Setting up your own newspaper is easy with *The Children's Writing and Publishing Center* or *The Writing Center,* both from The Learning Company, Fremont, California (IBM/Tandy & Compatibles, Macintosh®, Apple IIe/IIc/IIGS).

Writing Book Reviews

(pages 132-137)

Introduction

True readers *relish* book reviews because they love books and there's simply too much out there to read. Reviews help readers make decisions about the next books they will read. One reason bookstores across the country fill up on Sunday mornings is because readers are after the book review section of the *New York Times*! Our goal with this unit is to create that type of excitement with your young readers and writers.

Writing Book Reviews opens with a story about students in one classroom who really enjoy writing and sharing book reviews. The following pages contain an excellent student model, clear and simple writing guidelines, and a helpful collecting chart. The chapter ends with a special approach to writing a book review (a review with a special focus) and guidelines for writing in a reader response journal.

Rationale

- ***Book reviews give students opportunities to write about books they care about.***
- ***Book reviews give students opportunities to write persuasively.***
- ***Developing book reviews brings reading and writing skills together and demonstrates comprehension.***

Major Concepts

- ☐ **A book review provides an opportunity to respond to literature and to share this literature with others.** (page 132)
- ☐ **A basic book review answers three questions: (1) What is the book about? (2) What do I like about this book? (3) What is the book's theme or message?** (pages 134-135)

Planning Notes

MATERIALS NEEDED: A classroom filled with books, or a readily available collection of books in a library, is the most important consideration for implementing this unit.

READING/WRITING CONNECTIONS: Encourage students to write freely in their reader response journals about the books they read. (See page 137 for information about response journals.) Ideas in their response journals will help students write book reviews.

ACROSS-THE-CURRICULUM POSSIBILITIES: Students should be expected to write reviews for books that relate to all their course work.

Writing Explanations

(pages 138-141)

Introduction

Students are often called upon to write explanations, for many different reasons and in many different classes. In language arts, they may be asked to explain how to make something; in science, they may be asked to explain how a process works; in art, they may be asked to explain the steps they followed to complete a major project; and so on. Students may, in fact, be asked to write more explanations than any other form of writing throughout the curriculum.

The ***Writing Explanations*** chapter in the handbook provides all the information students need to develop effective explanations. The chapter includes clear and simple guidelines for the writing process and four excellent student models. Each model focuses on a different type of explanation: how to make something, how something works, how to get someplace, and how to create a feeling.

Rationale

- ***Writing explanations helps students write clearly and sequentially.***
- ***Writing explanations has practical applications that are easy for students to understand (giving directions, describing scientific processes, explaining experiments, and so on).***

Major Concepts

- ☐ **Explanations begin with a topic sentence (or a highly descriptive title), followed by clear, step-by-step directions.** (page 139)
- ☐ **The use of linking words (*first, next, then, finally,* etc.) makes explanations easier to follow.** (page 139)

Planning Notes

MATERIALS NEEDED: You might want to have several cookbooks (ones geared for kids have greater appeal) and science and invention books that describe how things work or how processes occur.

READING/WRITING CONNECTIONS: After reviewing the model explanations in the handbook, challenge students to find sample explanations in their favorite books or magazines. Here are two examples from books: The chapter entitled "Dance at Grandpa's" in Laura Ingalls Wilder's *Little House in the Big Woods* has a wonderful explanation for relieving the monotony of a pioneer winter. Betsy Byars's *Trouble River* gives a detailed explanation for making a raft.

ACROSS-THE-CURRICULUM POSSIBILITIES: Writing explanations can obviously play an important role in all aspects of the school curriculum. The introduction on this page suggests a few cross-curricular applications. You and your colleagues will think of many more.

Writing Business Letters

(pages 142-147)

Introduction

When students write business letters, they have the opportunity to express their concerns, request information, or attempt to solve a problem in a standard, businesslike way. They usually enjoy this form of writing for two reasons: It makes them feel like adults, and they enjoy receiving serious responses.

Writing Business Letters begins by explaining the difference between a friendly letter and a business letter; the three types of business letters are then described. The chapter explains the six parts of a business letter, identifying each part on a sample letter. Information about folding and sending letters is given, as well as a detailed checklist of the steps in this letter-writing process.

Rationale

- ***The business letter is a simple form that students can use to get action and recognition.***
- ***Students usually receive serious responses when their letters are carefully written. This helps them have faith in their abilities to effect change.***
- ***The ability to write a clear business letter will serve children now and throughout their lives.***

Major Concepts

- ☐ **The three types of business letters are a letter of request, a letter of complaint, and a letter to an editor or official.** (pages 142-143)
- ☐ **The business letter format includes the heading, inside address, salutation, body, closing, and signature.** (pages 144-145)
- ☐ **There is an accepted way to fold and address business letters.** (page 146)
- ☐ **Writing business letters involves using a writing process.** (page 147)

Planning Notes

MATERIALS NEEDED: Copies of local phone directories, newspapers, and other local publications will provide students with addresses and names of editors and businesspeople they may wish to contact.

READING/WRITING CONNECTIONS: Ask each student to choose a literary character who has a concern or complaint. Encourage your students to compose business letters from their characters' points of view. To make the letter credible, each student should gather pertinent details from the story in which the character appears. For fun, invite your students to read their letters to the class, omitting any reference to a character's name. Afterward, challenge the class to guess the identities of the characters.

ACROSS-THE-CURRICULUM POSSIBILITIES: Once they've learned the form, your class can do much of the business writing that has previously been your sole responsibility. They can invite visitors to the classroom, send letters of complaint if classroom materials aren't up to snuff, or write letters to the newspaper about local concerns.

Writing Observation Reports

(pages 148-151)

Introduction

Young people are natural observers. They notice everything around them, ask a lot of questions, and basically enjoy discovering the world around them. ***Writing Observation Reports*** taps into this natural ability, asking students to observe and write using all of their senses. This chapter takes young writers through the steps in the process of writing observation reports and provides two complete models.

Rationale

- ***Attention to detail is an important skill for young writers.***
- ***Observing and recording details of a scene give student writing greater fluency.***
- ***Improving observation skills is especially important in science classes.***

Major Concepts

- ☐ **Descriptive writing taps into all the senses.** (page 148)
- ☐ **Sensory details in writing enrich the reader's experience.** (pages 150-151)

Planning Notes

MATERIALS NEEDED: Your students might find a writing notebook or clipboard useful when the class is out and about. On the day you're going to begin this unit, bring in items that have interesting characteristics. Here are some suggestions: taste/smell items could be coffee, lemons, garlic, onions, and flowers; touch items could be fur, sandpaper, gravel, sand, silk, wood; sounds (inside and outside school) are ready to use, or you could bring in recordings.

READING/WRITING CONNECTIONS: After reading a book, students can choose one particular scene that they especially enjoyed and re-create it by writing an observation report from the character's point of view. Challenge them to write from memory. This will be your opportunity to discuss why some details are more memorable than others.

ACROSS-THE-CURRICULUM POSSIBILITIES: As seen in the student model on page 151, observation reports are a natural fit with writing and reporting in science. The use of all the senses will make the observations more vivid, and a clear record of the details observed will help students reach valid conclusions.

Writing Fantasies

(pages 153-159)

Introduction

"Impossible things? Let's pretend. Make-believe. What would happen if? I wish I were . . . I wish I had . . . . Those words are the starting place for millions of stories!" says Nancy Bond, author of many popular fantasies.

Writing Fantasies, which is based on Bond's work, opens with a series of questions that remind your students they create fantasies all the time. After reading the student model, your children will be drawn into the author's process. As Bond talks about her notebook and how she asks questions and makes choices, her story begins to unfold in front of their eyes. Next, your students are given guidelines for prewriting, drafting, revising, editing, and proofreading their own fantasies.

Rationale

- ***When writing fantasy, young writers have permission to develop characters, problems, and solutions exactly to their liking.***
- ***The essence of life for fifth graders is change. Because so many fantasies involve transformations, this form seems a natural choice for this age group.***
- ***In fantasy, students can explore some of the great themes in literature: the struggle between good and evil, the ability to overcome obstacles with faith and perseverance, and the power of love and friendship.***

Major Concepts

- ☐ **In fantasy stories anything can happen, as long as it's believable.** (page 153)
- ☐ **Writing stories involves asking questions and making choices.** (pages 156-157)
- ☐ **A fantasy needs characters, a problem, and a setting.** (page 158)
- ☐ **Revising involves time away from a story, a chance to make certain it's believable, and the opportunity to share a draft and get feedback.** (page 159)

Planning Notes

HANDBOOK CONSIDERATIONS: In this unit we recommend that each student keep a writer's notebook

READING/WRITING CONNECTIONS: Two read-alouds to consider are *Inside My Feet: The Story of a Giant* by Richard Kennedy and *A String in the Harp* by Nancy Bond.

ACROSS-THE-CURRICULUM POSSIBILITIES: Because fantasies, especially transformation tales, involve change, watch for transformation possibilities in science, math, and social studies. For example, in science, children may chronicle the development of mealworms, tadpoles, or seeds. Books about individuals who reverse damage done to our natural world are appropriate read-alouds (*Waterman's Boy* by Susan Sharp or *A River Ran Wild* by Lynne Cherry).

Writing Tall Tales

(pages 160-163)

Introduction

None of us would be hard-pressed to name a time when we exaggerated to make a point. Remember the "big fish" story—the one that goes "I caught a fish the likes of which you won't believe!"—told with arms stretched out at least two feet? Fortunately, the human tendency to exaggerate serves the tall-tale writer well.

Writing Tall Tales exhibits two particular characteristics: blatant exaggeration and humor. In the midst of this exaggeration, however, there is often an element of reason and believability—enough to keep our attention. For example, the reader who learns about Pecos Bill riding a cyclone later learns that after the ride, he has trouble dismounting safely. This blend of exaggeration and reason makes tall tales appealing to all ages.

Rationale

- ***Tall-tale writing gives students' imaginations free rein.***
- ***The necessity for exaggeration and humor entices even reluctant writers.***
- ***In tall tales, students are able to control both good and evil. Children at this age have a strong need to feel this sort of power.***

Major Concepts

- ☐ **Tall tales incorporate exaggeration and humor.** (pages 160-163)
- ☐ **Tall tales require especially descriptive language. Studying and using figures of speech (especially similes) are integral to writing tall tales.** (page 162)

Planning Notes

MATERIALS NEEDED: Having collections of tall tales for students to read would be beneficial during this unit.

READING/WRITING CONNECTIONS: Because this form of literature is enjoyable for students to read, it would be a good time to use small-group reading circles. Any full-length version of *Paul Bunyan* or *Iva Dunnit and the Big Wind* by Carol Purdy would make an excellent read-aloud. (Also see "Literature Link" on page 163 in the handbook.)

ACROSS-THE-CURRICULUM POSSIBILITIES: Tall tales are part of our nation's oral history, so you can make connections between tall tales and events in history. Two possibilities include the stories about John Henry and the expansion of the railroad and about Paul Bunyan and the lumber industry. Three fine collections of tales of all types are *The Kingdom Under the Sea and Other Stories* by Joan Aiken, *The Elephant's Bathtub: Wonder Tales from the Far East* by Frances Carpenter, and *American Indian Myths and Legends* edited by Richard Erdoes and Alfonso Ortiz.

Writing Realistic Stories

(pages 164-169)

Introduction

Anything's possible in realistic fiction as long as it seems true, could be true, but hasn't actually happened. Author Sandy Asher says, "In realistic fiction, characters find their own realistic solutions. And their search teaches them—and their readers—something worth knowing about real life. Realistic fiction isn't about facts, but it is about truth."

To help students better understand this story form, the opening page of ***Writing Realistic Stories*** introduces them to Amanda Lowe, a fictional character with a real problem. (Amanda makes many additional appearances in the chapter.) On the following pages, students will also find a model realistic story and detailed writing guidelines, covering everything from creating a character to adding life to a story.

Rationale

- ***Writing realistic stories helps students better understand the fiction-writing process.***
- ***Writing realistic stories helps students appreciate that ideas for writing can come from their own lives.***

Major Concepts

- ☐ **The characters and problems in realistic fiction may be based on real life.** (pages 164-166)
- ☐ **It helps to think about the main elements in a story before writing.** (page 167)
- ☐ **There are several exciting ways to start a realistic story.** (page 168)
- ☐ **Realistic characters solve their problems in believable ways.** (page 168)
- ☐ **Specific details, dialogue, and action add life to stories.** (page 169)

Planning Notes

READING/WRITING CONNECTIONS: Excerpts from realistic fiction might be shared aloud on a daily basis. Some of the most popular authors for this age are Judy Blume, Bill Brittain, Clyde Robert Bulla, Betsy Byars, Beverly Cleary, Matt Christopher, Paula Danziger, Jamie Gilson, Lois Lowry, Patricia MacLachlan, Norma Fox Mazer, Robert Newton Peck, Susan Pfeffer, and Cynthia Rylant.

ACROSS-THE-CURRICULUM POSSIBILITIES: Writing realistic fiction is a way for students to expand their knowledge in different subject areas. For example, a student could choose to write a story about someone in a particular profession, like a wildlife biologist, or about someone living in a foreign country. Writing such a story would require specialized knowledge gained through research.

Writing Stories from History

(pages 170-175)

Introduction

The writer of historical stories aims to tell a tale set in a past time. The tale must be believable to be interesting, and so it must be founded in the truth about a particular time, or at least in what could have been the truth—what could have happened based on the circumstances of a certain period. This kind of writing has the potential for making history truly interesting to students. As they create characters and action that fit into a historically accurate setting, history becomes more relevant and real.

Writing Stories from History guides students through the process of exploring a period in history, then writing a story from that era. Students start by getting into a historical mind-set, then continue by listing ideas, gathering facts, and planning a story. (Historical stories share the same elements as realistic stories, so it may be helpful to review pages 164-169 in the handbook before beginning.)

Rationale

- ***Writing stories from history requires students to delve into history, exploring a person, an era, or an event.***
- ***The study of history becomes more real and more interesting for students as they read about a period and then write stories from history.***

Major Concepts

- ☐ **Historical stories may be about real characters or about made-up characters who could have lived during a certain time.** (page 171)
- ☐ **Collecting accurate information about the historical period (and about real characters) can be achieved by reading and by talking with teachers and librarians.** (page 172)
- ☐ **Identifying the main elements in a story before writing the first draft is important.** (page 173)
- ☐ **Blending historical facts (setting, clothing, food, work, homes, real events, etc.) with fictional elements (words a character could have said, daily events that could have happened considering the period, etc.) will make the story believable.** (page 175)

Planning Notes

MATERIALS NEEDED: This lesson involves lots of digging on the part of the students, so having a variety of reference materials available will be beneficial.

READING/WRITING CONNECTIONS: Choose one historical fiction book to read aloud, and take time to do book talks about some of your favorite titles. As students research to write their stories, especially when reading nonfiction sources for information, the reading strategies on pages 238-243 of the handbook will help.

ACROSS-THE-CURRICULUM POSSIBILITIES: Your students could dress in costumes of the era and give dramatic readings of their stories. You could create a time line or ask students to make posters that highlight the important events and people of the eras they've chosen to write about. Put the posters up in correct time order and have students take a stroll through history.

Writing Poems

(pages 177-187)

Introduction

Writing Poems begins with an invitation to make friends with poetry. Anne-Marie Oomen then invites students to think about what makes poetry special. After this puzzle is solved, students are guided through the steps for writing free-verse poetry. The chapter continues with definitions and examples of figures of speech and poetic devices for creating effective images and sounds in poetry. Finally, helpful lists of traditional and invented poetry types are provided.

Rationale

- ***Writing poetry gives students an opportunity to better understand this form of writing.***
- ***Writing poetry offers students a personal and creative avenue for exploring and expressing their ideas.***
- ***Students learn to choose words purposefully.***
- ***Students come to understand that sounds of words and figures of speech help to convey meaning.***

Major Concepts

- ☐ **Poets often speak from personal experience.** (pages 177-180)
- ☐ **The language of poetry is keen and alive.** (page 181)
- ☐ **Poets often use figures of speech.** (page 182)
- ☐ **The sound of poetry is important.** (page 183)
- ☐ **There are many types of poems.** (pages 184-187)

Planning Notes

RELATED MATERIALS: Because this chapter introduces many types of poems, having examples of poems visible in the classroom will nurture student curiosity.

READING/WRITING CONNECTIONS: Reading poetry throughout this unit is almost a necessity. Terrific read-alouds include *Somebody Catch My Homework* by David Harrison; *If You're Not Here, Please Raise Your Hand* by Kalli Dakos; and *Through Our Eyes: Poems and Pictures About Growing Up* selected by Lee Bennett Hopkins.

Writing Songs

(pages 188-191)

Introduction

Well before they can talk, children create singsong rhythms and sounds. It's a natural, universal "language." Through their early years, students chant their own versions of nursery rhymes, favorite poems, and, nowadays, advertisements. So when Charles Temple, the major contributor to this chapter, asks students if they've ever wanted to write a song, we suspect he knows the answer will probably be a resounding, "Yes!"

Writing Songs opens with an invitation to try another creative form of writing—the song. It outlines step-by-step the songwriting process. The chapter ends with a "Songwriter's Toolbox," which lists standard reference books for songwriters, including a rhyming dictionary.

Rationale

- ***Writing songs provides another creative-writing outlet.***
- ***The process of making up verses and passing them along allows children to participate in a kind of communication that people have shared for thousands of years.***

Major Concepts

- ☐ **After you get an idea for the first line, the rhythm and rhyme pattern in an existing song can suggest a "frame" for writing a new song.** (pages 188-189)
- ☐ **Songs often include refrains.** (page 189)
- ☐ **Songs need organization, with a beginning, a middle, and an end.** (page 190)
- ☐ **Songwriters often use standard reference books as well as rhyming dictionaries to write verses.** (page 191)

Planning Notes

MATERIALS NEEDED: You might need a tape recorder. If you're unfamiliar with the song "Frog Went a Courtin'," ask your school's music teacher for a record, tape, or CD of the song. A rhyming dictionary can also be helpful.

READING/WRITING CONNECTIONS: Study folk songs—work songs, freedom songs, war songs, peace songs, love songs, riddle songs, game songs, dance songs—to stimulate interest in this songwriting chapter. Good sources of folk songs are Carl Sandburg's *American Songbag*, John Lomax's *Folk Songs of North America,* and a recent book from Sing Out Publications called *Rise Up Singing*.

ACROSS-THE-CURRICULUM POSSIBILITIES: Songs translate well into artwork. Let your students make several drawings to illustrate the content of a song. Then do a "roller show" of images, if you choose. Attach the drawings to one another in sequence, and then attach the ends to sticks. Ask for two volunteers to unwind the pictures while the students sing the song.

Writing Plays

(pages 192-197)

Introduction

No matter who is writing a play, a fifth grader or a professional writer, the basic elements are the same: A main character solves a problem or reaches an important goal through action.

Writing Plays begins with a simple definition ("A play is really a story in dialogue form") and then shows students how Sandy Asher presents the *problem* and shapes the *action* in the opening scene of "What Will We Tell Mom and Dad?" The chapter continues with instructions for students to write their own plays, including prewriting plans, tips for writing the first draft, and revision tips. The chapter ends by showing how a student writer chose to continue Asher's play in "Scene II."

Rationale

- ***When writing plays, children learn about the use of language, the logical progression of ideas, the consequences of behavior, role playing, and group dynamics.***
- ***Writing plays sustains the life of the imagination.***
- ***Young people's theater can lead to a love of drama.***

Major Concepts

- ☐ **Plays begin with characters who need to solve a problem or want to reach a goal.** (pages 193-194)
- ☐ **A writer's first task is to introduce the characters and their situation to the audience. This is usually done through dialogue.** (pages 193-194)
- ☐ **Writers often discover how a play will progress as they write.** (page 194)
- ☐ **When writing plays, authors have the challenge of solving problems, but not too quickly. Excitement and fun can be created as characters get in one another's way.** (page 195)
- ☐ **The ending of a play shows how things finally work out.** (page 195)
- ☐ **Plays make a *point*. As young authors write and revise, this *point* (theme) helps them decide what to keep and what to put aside.** (page 196)

Planning Notes

RELATED MATERIALS: A tape recorder is useful for testing out dialogue. Students can read their scripts aloud, play back the results, and revise as necessary.

READING/WRITING CONNECTIONS: The more plays children read, the better idea they'll have of what a play looks like on paper. Look for plays in your school library, especially in the magazine, fairy-tale, tall-tale, and fable sections.

ACROSS-THE-CURRICULUM POSSIBILITIES: Classroom reports have *play* potential because so much in our world revolves around solving problems or reaching goals—the building of the first transcontinental railroad, surviving the Oregon Trail, the need for solar energy. Your students might present their report assignments in play form. Groups working on related topics could write a play together.

Writing Riddles

(pages 198-201)

Introduction

What makes riddles fun and often funny? Riddle writers say it's wordplay—words playing with one another and with you. Along with a lot of imagination, this unit offers several ways students can play with words to make riddles. Students will go wild searching for puns, outlandish metaphors, and words to personify things they never dreamed of.

Writing Riddles describes this kind of writing not only as fun but as a form of mental exercise. Students are taken step-by-step through the writing process for "crack up" riddles (using puns) and "what am I" riddles (using metaphor and personification).

Rationale

- ***Students this age are ripe for discovering the fun of writing riddles.***
- ***Writing riddles gives students a creative outlet for using puns and figures of speech.***
- ***Working with riddles is a form of mental exercise.***
- ***Writing riddles increases vocabulary.***

Major Concepts

- **Telling riddles is a form of mental exercise.** (page 198)
- **Writing riddles can incorporate homonyms, homographs, and two figures of speech—personification and metaphor**. (pages 199-200)
- **Students write riddles by following specific steps.** (pages 199-201)

Planning Notes

MATERIALS NEEDED: "Using the Right Word," pages 362-369 in the handbook, will prove invaluable as students write "crack up" riddles. Also have a variety of riddle books available in the classroom.

READING/WRITING CONNECTIONS: Reading and sharing riddles is probably the best way for students to get into the spirit of riddle writing. Don't miss *Funny You Should Ask: How to Make Up Jokes and Riddles with Wordplay; Hey, Hay! A Wagonful of Funny Homonym Riddles;* and *Eight Ate: A Feast of Homonym Riddles*—all by Marvin Terban. *What's a Frank Frank? Tasty Homograph Riddles* by Giulio Maestro is another fine collection.

ACROSS-THE-CURRICULUM POSSIBILITIES: In *Raps and Rhymes in Math,* Ann and Johnny Baker suggest that if we really want to know how students feel about a subject, we need to encourage them to talk about it. Riddles can lead to informal discussions in which students "feel able to express with honesty, and in the security of a friendly group, exactly what their attitude . . . is." We strongly urge you to employ riddle writing across the curriculum, not only to gauge attitude, but for all the fun it provides.

Writing for Fun

(pages 202-205)

Introduction

Since we spend so much time and effort helping students to learn how to write, it's a relief to come back to the premise that one can simply "write for fun" (no grading necessary!). In ***Writing for Fun,*** Peter Stillman, a major contributor to this chapter, shares many engaging suggestions that get students involved in the enjoyment of writing. He begins with ideas for family stories, then explains storyboarding and writing playful poems—two of the more enjoyable ways of writing for fun!

Rationale

- ***Discovering that writing is fun helps establish good writing habits in students.***
- ***Students' daily lives contain all the subject matter they need to fill a writing-for-fun notebook.***
- ***Writing family stories for fun facilitates communication among family members and heightens personal-history awareness.***
- ***Writing is an activity that students can do anywhere every day for the rest of their lives.***

Major Concepts

- ☐ **Writing is a fun, inexpensive hobby.** (page 202)
- ☐ **Family life provides rich writing material.** (page 203)
- ☐ **Storyboards help writers order the elements of their stories as well as add the creative touch of pictures.** (page 204)
- ☐ **Writing poetry can be playful and amusing.** (pages 204-205)

Using the Library

(pages 207-215)

Introduction

Research . . . ugh! Library work . . . no way! Have any of us ever gotten these responses from a student, or two, or three? Fear of the unknown can prompt such reactions. Students may know where to find their favorite mysteries or sports stories, while information on the constellations or volcanoes eludes them. As teachers, we must encourage a friendly "relationship" between the library and our students so they can find out for themselves what a valuable place it is. Familiarity is a key factor.

Using the Library thoroughly covers the main steps in using the card catalog, finding a book on the shelf, using a computer catalog, and using the encyclopedia as well as other reference books. It also explains how to use the *Children's Magazine Guide,* a handy research tool for young students.

Rationale

- ***Libraries, whether on-line or not, continue to be storehouses of knowledge that students need to access.***
- ***Knowing how to find and use the library's resources is an invaluable skill for all students.***
- ***Familiarity with the library will help to ensure its productive use.***

Major Concepts

- ☐ **The library is a place for students to "meet" experts and "hear" their stories through books, magazines, computers, videos, and so on.** (page 207)
- ☐ **Knowing how to use the card catalog (in libraries that still use them) will help students find specific books.** (pages 208-209)
- ☐ **Understanding the arrangement of books by call numbers, authors' last names (fiction), or subjects' last names (biographies) will help students find specific books on the shelves.** (page 210)
- ☐ **In many libraries, the computer catalog will help students find specific books.** (page 211)
- ☐ **The encyclopedia (book form or CD) serves as a starting place for finding general information on any topic.** (page 212)
- ☐ **Many kinds of reference books (dictionaries, atlases, biographical, first facts, etc.) in the library contain interesting, up-to-date information.** (page 213)
- ☐ **Understanding the parts of reference books will help students use them efficiently.** (page 214)
- ☐ **The *Children's Magazine Guide* can help students find recent articles on chosen subjects.** (page 215)

Writing a Summary

(pages 216-219)

Introduction

When students write summaries, they are learning how to identify the main ideas in reading material and how to present these ideas in clear and simple mini-reports. Summarizing is a very effective writing-to-learn technique, one that helps students personalize—or internalize—learning, so they understand better and remember longer.

Writing a Summary begins with a rationale for learning how to summarize and a clear definition of the form. A model is given, along with the text from which it was derived. Then students are led through a step-by-step approach to summary writing. Finally, the handbook lists helpful hints for finding the main idea in writing material.

Rationale

- ***Summarizing helps students process information.***
- ***The ability to write summaries will help students develop longer pieces of writing, including book reviews, classroom reports, and news stories.***
- ***Writing summaries promotes higher level thinking skills.***

Major Concepts

- ☐ **Summarizing is easier for students if they read and write with a plan in mind.** (page 218)
- ☐ **Summaries need to be stated in the writer's own words.** (page 218)
- ☐ **The structure of a summary is much like a paragraph, with a topic sentence and supporting details.** (page 218)

Planning Notes

READING/WRITING CONNECTIONS: Choose a selection of popular books with good book-jacket summaries. Read several of these summaries aloud to the class, and discuss the purpose they serve. As a class, compose a summary for a book that everyone has recently read. Then invite your students to write book-jacket summaries for some of their favorite books. Publish these summaries in a class notebook.

ACROSS-THE-CURRICULUM POSSIBILITIES: Whenever students have to process large amounts of information—no matter if they are reading a challenging chapter in a science text or reviewing for a unit test in history—they should be encouraged to summarize their learning material.

Writing a Classroom Report

(pages 220-233)

Introduction

A report is a collection of facts and other information (such as true stories and quotations) about a selected topic. A report might focus on elephants for a classroom anthology about our natural world, or it might be one of a series of student-made booklets on electricity for a classroom library. A well-written report is interesting, clear, and accurate.

In ***Writing a Classroom Report,*** students will learn about the complete report-writing process—from limiting a topic to collecting information, from writing a first draft to editing and proofreading the final copy. The skills that your students practice here will help them with their report writing in all of their subjects, now and for years to come.

Rationale

- ***Writing reports will help students understand how nonfiction can be organized.***
- ***Many students will have to write nonfiction as adults. Developing report-writing skills now will prepare them for these types of tasks.***
- ***Students are naturally curious, and when they are allowed to choose their own topics, they find report writing interesting and enjoyable.***

Major Concepts

- ☐ **Students should research topics of personal interest.** (pages 220-222)
- ☐ **Selecting a topic should be a thoughtful process.** (pages 222-223)
- ☐ **A report should answer questions the writer wants answered.** (page 224)
- ☐ **Using gathering grids and note cards can help students organize information.** (pages 225-227)
- ☐ **Reports require good beginnings.** (page 228)
- ☐ **The facts found in the body of a report must be tied together.** (page 229)

Planning Notes

HANDBOOK CONSIDERATIONS: This chapter will require time in the library for research and plenty of paper for gathering grids and drafting.

READING/WRITING CONNECTIONS: Have your students suggest nonfiction titles for the class to read, or make your own favorite titles available. As the class reads nonfiction selections, discuss the following points about writing reports: (1) authors usually choose *part* of a larger topic to write about; (2) authors organize their information in different ways (time sequence, a series of questions); (3) authors' choices and the ways in which they present details vary (some use description, others depend on comparisons or a straightforward cataloging of facts; (4) an author's tone can be serious or lighthearted.

The Tools of Learning

"The Tools of Learning" will help students improve all of their study and learning skills. Included in this section of the handbook are chapters on reading, vocabulary, speaking, thinking, working in groups, test taking, and much more. There are even guidelines for reading pictures and performing poems. The table of contents below lists all of the chapters in "The Tools of Learning" section of the handbook. The page numbers refer to the location of each chapter summary in this guide.

Special Note: For minilessons related to learning tools, see pages 103-107.

Improving Your Reading

Improving Your Spelling and Vocabulary

Improving Your Speaking and Listening

Improving Your Thinking

Improving Your Learning Skills

Using Reading Strategies

(pages 237-245)

Introduction

Reading comprehension involves an active reader—one who is able to accommodate new information and determine the concepts in the text that are important. Because reading is a strategic process, it means that during any reading event, thoughtful readers tend to draw from prior knowledge, interact with the information in the text, and create their own personal and unique meaning for the material.

Using Reading Strategies offers students tools to continue their progress toward becoming interactive, thoughtful readers. The chapter begins with a plan of action: read often, read everything, change your speed as you read, and use reading strategies. The last item on the list, "use reading strategies," comprises most of the chapter's content. Students will find an explanation of several reading strategies for fiction and nonfiction. The chapter ends with definitions of literary terms.

Rationale

- ***Students will learn new strategies or practices to help them become more active and thoughtful readers.***
- ***Many students are capable readers, but, at times, they do not carry out their reading tasks in an efficient manner. For example, they may spend excessive time decoding proper nouns, fail to use context clues to get meaning, or neglect to vary their speed while reading.***

Major Concepts

- ☐ **Reading is an interactive process. It takes place when a reader actively engages with a text and creates meaning.** (pages 238-245)
- ☐ **There are many strategies for comprehending a text, and good readers use them before, during, and after reading.** (pages 238-239)
- ☐ **Strategies are tools for reading effectively and efficiently.** (pages 239-243)
- ☐ **Reading strategies can be modeled/taught/learned in the context of classroom reading instruction.** (pages 237-243)

Reading Pictures

(pages 246-253)

Introduction

"Reading pictures" means understanding symbols, signs, graphs, and other kinds of pictures that convey information. Information pictures, such as hieroglyphics, are among the oldest forms of written communication. They are also among the newest. Graphs, which are nonrepresentational pictures of information, were invented only about 200 years ago.

Reading Pictures begins with two examples of how pictures have been used to communicate at different times and places. Students are then introduced to the most common kinds of information pictures: signs and symbols, diagrams, graphs, and tables.

Rationale

- ***Students must learn how to interpret commonly used forms of written communication. Newspapers, magazines, advertisements, and TV news programs use graphs, tables, symbols, and other information pictures.***
- ***The skills needed to "read" visually presented information differ from those needed to read verbal information.***

Major Concepts

- ☐ **Pictures are not always just decoration; they can be a form of written communication.** (page 246)
- ☐ **One of the advantages of communicating with pictures rather than words is that a picture can mean the same thing to everyone.** (page 246)
- ☐ **The most basic type of information picture is a sign or symbol.** (page 247)
- ☐ **A diagram is like a map of an object or a set of objects.** (page 248)
- ☐ **A graph is a picture of information rather than a picture of objects; that is, graphs are nonrepresentational pictures.** (pages 249-251)
- ☐ **A table uses rows and columns to show how different kinds of information relate to one another.** (pages 252-253)

Building Vocabulary Skills

(pages 255-269)

Introduction

A basic part of the process of education is learning the meanings of new words. Students will become better independent learners if they have a desire to learn new words. Also, the stronger their vocabulary, the more they will get out of what they read and hear.

Building Vocabulary Skills begins by encouraging students to become more wordwise. The strategies for learning new words are aimed at helping students become independent learners. "Read, read, read!" comes first because inferring the meanings of unfamiliar words in text is a major avenue of vocabulary growth. The remaining five strategies include using context clues, keeping a vocabulary notebook, using a thesaurus, using a dictionary, and studying word parts and forms. Students are given three useful charts that list prefixes, suffixes, and common word roots.

Rationale

- ***Vocabulary knowledge is fundamental to reading comprehension; one cannot understand text without knowing what most of the words mean.***
- ***Knowing several strategies for increasing one's vocabulary enables students to become independent learners.***

Major Concepts

- ☐ **Reading is the most effective word-learning strategy.** (page 256)
- ☐ **There are several ways to use context when figuring out the meanings of new words.** (page 256)
- ☐ **Vocabulary notebooks are most useful when they include definitions and examples.** (page 256)
- ☐ **Tools such as thesauruses and dictionaries in the home, classroom, and library should be available to help learners.** (pages 257-258)
- ☐ **Knowing the meanings of word parts (prefixes, suffixes, and roots) helps people figure out the meanings of new words.** (page 260)

Becoming a Better Speller

(pages 270-273)

Introduction and Rationale

"Spelling as a subject ranks just below reading and mathematics as a national priority." So says Donald Graves in *Writing: Teachers & Children at Work* when he cites a national survey given to parents. We, too, feel spelling is important, but not as a separate subject or an end unto itself. As you will see in these notes, we closely tie spelling instruction to learning to write and read.

In general, we want our students to spell an ever-growing number of words correctly and automatically when they write. In rough drafts or journal entries, we want to see risks taken with words they use orally but aren't sure how to spell. We also want our students to learn how to find the correct spelling of a word. And when they are proofreading, we hope our students care about spelling for the correct reason: readability of their work.

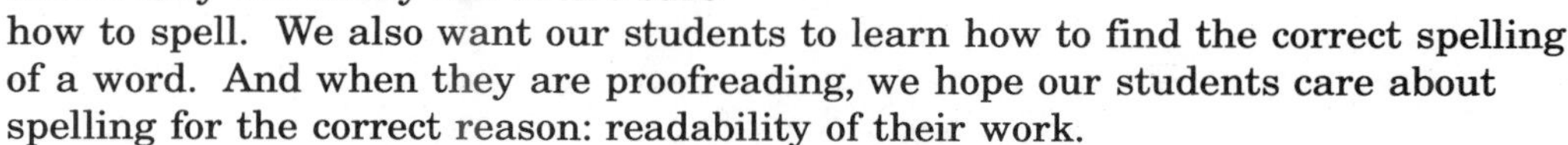

When they are reading, we want students to notice common letter patterns and the positional constraints of some letters and letter clusters. We want them to recognize and understand new words that are simply derivations of common roots they know. We hope, too, that they will use analogy to pronounce unknown words, and that they will become sensitive to how words look on the page.

Becoming a Better Speller is a self-help guide for students. The chapter includes ideas for making a spelling dictionary, strategies for remembering challenging spellings, a guide to proofreading for spelling, and a number of basic spelling rules.

Major Concepts

- ☐ **There are strategies students can use to become better spellers.** (pages 270-273)
- ☐ **It helps to use all the senses when learning to spell.** (page 271)
- ☐ **Proofreading for spelling is part of the writing process.** (page 272)
- ☐ **Knowing a few basic rules can help students avoid common errors.** (page 273)

Giving Speeches

(pages 275-281)

Introduction

Giving a talk, presentation, or formal speech is a skill students will find useful throughout their lives. Whether they find themselves before the student council asking for a new bike rack at school or before the city council arguing for a new bike path, students who have some understanding and experience in giving speeches will find situations like these less daunting. This chapter introduces students to the building blocks of speech making.

Giving Speeches begins with the author's story about her growing willingness to speak to a group. The author then talks to the students about the importance of picking the right topic and suggests they ask themselves a basic question: "Why am I giving this speech?" This question naturally leads into a discussion of the types of speeches and the kinds of topics suitable for each, which is followed by a discussion of the eight steps in a speech-writing process. The chapter ends with Angela Zischke's speech about living in Lansing, Michigan.

Rationale

- ***Training in public speaking prepares students for leadership roles.***
- ***As students narrow topics for their speeches, they learn to think about an audience and its relationship to their speech's purpose, topic, and tone.***
- ***Because most students enjoy talking about things they know a great deal about, learning to give speeches can be a highly enjoyable educational experience.***
- ***Students discover that the same skills and strategies can be used for different purposes. Creating a speech is much like writing a report.***

Major Concepts

- ☐ **Choosing a speech topic is a personal and thoughtful process.** (page 276)
- ☐ **There are three types of speeches listed in *Writers Express:* informative, demonstrative, and persuasive.** (page 276)
- ☐ **One speech-writing process involves the eight steps listed in *Writers Express.*** (pages 276-280)

Planning Notes

MATERIALS NEEDED: If you ask students to prepare their outlines on note cards, they will need a supply of them. Some students will need props or visual aids to accompany their speeches. For practicing and polishing a speech, an audio- or videotape recorder may come in handy.

READING/WRITING/SPEAKING CONNECTIONS: Written reports in any subject provide content for speeches. And because speeches are often shorter than reports read aloud, they can keep your wiggly students' attention.

ACROSS-THE-CURRICULUM POSSIBILITIES: The content of almost every discipline can be used as speech material. Social studies often offers some exciting chances for students to practice their speaking and citizenship skills before different audiences. Encourage your students to write persuasive speeches to effect changes in your community. School-board meetings, for instance, usually encourage student input.

Performing Poems

(pages 282-287)

Introduction

Allan Wolf, a major contributor to this chapter, loosely defines poetry performance as the process of moving poetry from the page to the stage. Students get on their feet, individually and in teams, to present poetry skits on a stage or at the front of the classroom. The primary concern is with *how* the poetry is presented rather than with *what* the poetry is saying. Even so, students do have to understand the poetry in order to perform it.

Performing Poems begins with a story about Melinda Castillo, a young poet who's written about spring. She isn't sure what to do with her poem now that it's written. One answer is poetry performance. The chapter outlines five steps in the performance process: form a team, find a poem, script the poem, score the poem, and perform the poem. (Memorization should be encouraged, though *not* required. Memorizing allows for more focused performances and leaves the students with poems in their heads.) The chapter ends by inviting students to script and score "The Salmon People," a poem written by Native American students from Beverly Elementary School.

Rationale

- ***To bring poetry to life, students must read, hear, and speak the poetry.***
- ***By performing it, students will understand and relate to poetry in a way not possible through the solitary act of reading it silently.***
- ***Performance encourages both participatory and cooperative learning.***
- ***Poetry performance culminates in actual presentation that gives students a sense of purpose and accomplishment.***
- ***As students take their performances elsewhere, they learn how to conduct themselves in front of groups.***

Planning Notes

MATERIALS NEEDED: Collect as many poetry books as possible and have them available in the classroom. A tape recorder comes in handy for those interested in memorizing their poems.

READING/WRITING CONNECTIONS: Have a poetry break in your class as often as possible. Each day, without warning, hold up a sign that reads "POETRY BREAK!" All students stop what they are doing to listen to and watch a presentation. Encourage the presentation of old favorites as well as original poetry written by your students.

ACROSS-THE-CURRICULUM POSSIBILITIES: Poetry has been written on every subject imaginable. Epic poems that deal with a historical subject or myth often lend themselves to group readings. Poems about nature can be incorporated into a science lesson. And why not shake up your math class with a poem about mathematics?

Improving Viewing Skills

(pages 288-291)

Introduction

Television plays a major role in shaping what children know and believe about the world. The average child spends much more time with TV than with parents. And some kids spend as much time with TV as they do in school! That means that children need to be educated viewers of television.

Improving Viewing Skills helps students become more discerning viewers of TV news programs and education specials. The first page of the chapter notes how much time Americans spend with television and that most of that time is spent watching entertainment, not informational, programs. On the next page, a story that students will relate to illustrates how news programs are made and why they don't always show things exactly as they happened. The final pages offer questions and guidelines for intelligent viewing of both the news and educational specials.

Rationale

- ***Most students are unaware of how TV news is shaped by the people who present it—reporters, camera people, editors, producers, and so on—and how this shaping process can sometimes lead to bias.***
- ***Students need to know how to assess the news programs that shape their understanding of the world.***
- ***Students will learn more from educational programs if they follow a few simple viewing guidelines.***

Major Concepts

- ☐ **Television is one of the most powerful influences in students' lives (some say *the* most powerful).** (page 288)
- ☐ **TV news does not show things exactly as they happen; it shows only a part of the big picture.** (page 289)
- ☐ **Students need to watch the news with a questioning attitude, to make sure it meets certain standards of completeness and fairness.** (page 290)
- ☐ **Students can learn more from educational programs by viewing them thoughtfully and actively.** (page 291)

Improving Listening Skills

(pages 292-293)

Introduction

Students spend more time listening than they do speaking, reading, and writing combined. With that much "practice," you might expect students to automatically develop good listening skills. But, of course, they don't. With practice, however, students can learn how to listen effectively.

Improving Listening Skills points out that listening is more than just hearing—it involves the mind as well as the ears. The checklist of good listening skills provides specific tips for effective listening.

Rationale

- ***Many students are unaware of the difference between hearing and listening.***
- ***Good listening skills help students learn better and faster.***
- ***Good listening skills help students become more successful, not only in the classroom but also in their personal relationships and in their lives outside school.***

Major Concepts

- ☐ **Listening is more than just hearing—it is an active mental process.** (page 292)
- ☐ **Good listeners listen with their eyes as well as their ears, and they listen with a good attitude.** (page 293)
- ☐ **Active listening means listening for specific things: directions, main ideas, key words, and the speaker's tone of voice.** (page 293)
- ☐ **Active listening means *doing* certain things: taking notes, making drawings, relating what's being said to other knowledge, and picturing what is said.** (page 293)

Getting Organized

(pages 295-299)

Introduction

Graphic organizers are spatial (lists and outlines) or pictorial (Venn diagrams) approaches to writing down ideas. Listing, asking questions, making diagrams, and outlining will help your students get their ideas down on paper so they can be rearranged, rewritten, or set aside.

Getting Organized begins with a rationale for becoming a better, more organized thinker. Five types of graphic organizers follow, which are meant to help students accomplish their "getting organized" tasks. Then the handbook asks students to think about seven other ways in which they can become better learners.

Rationale

- ***Graphic organizers are excellent tools for organizing and studying information.***
- ***Students need specific information and advice on how to become better learners.***

Major Concepts

- ☐ **To think well, students have to be able to gather details and organize them in a way that makes sense.** (page 295)
- ☐ **Graphic organizers are shapes created from lines, circles, and boxes that help you collect and organize details.** (page 296)
- ☐ **Becoming organized isn't easy, but it can be done.** (page 298)
- ☐ **Observing, gathering, questioning, organizing, imagining, rethinking, and evaluating are helpful strategies for gathering and organizing thoughts.** (page 299)

Thinking and Writing

(pages 300-307)

Introduction

It's impossible to produce good writing without good thinking. A vast vocabulary and a flawless command of grammar will result in technically correct nonsense if they're not used to express sound thinking.

Thinking and Writing begins by pointing out that thinking is the foundation of all academic skills, including reading, writing, and speaking. (Of course, sound thinking is as necessary to success in life as it is to success in school.) The chapter goes on to explain six kinds of thinking and how students can use them in their writing. Models are included. Finally, the information is summarized in a chart called "Guidelines for Thinking and Writing."

Rationale

- ***Students need to be aware that thinking skills are as essential to good writing as mechanics and sentence structure.***
- ***Students need to learn different ways of thinking and how to use them in their writing.***
- ***Good thinking skills and an awareness of the different kinds of thinking will help students meet challenges inside and outside the classroom.***

Major Concepts

- ☐ **Thinking is the foundation of all other classroom skills.** (page 300)
- ☐ **Students can, and must, "learn" to think.** (page 300)
- ☐ **There are six general categories of thinking: recalling, understanding, applying, analyzing, synthesizing, and evaluating.** (page 300)

Thinking Clearly

(pages 308-313)

Introduction

As children grow, we ask them to work on organizing their thoughts more clearly. Specific strategies that often involve writing can help students become even better thinkers.

Thinking Clearly begins with a discussion about the thinking process. Four strategies for improving thinking skills follow: using facts and opinions correctly, avoiding fuzzy thinking, making good decisions, and solving problems.

Rationale

- ***Students must learn the difference between facts and opinions.***
- ***When students learn to avoid the pitfalls of fuzzy thinking, they will find it easier to express themselves clearly.***
- ***Students need strategies for making good decisions and solving problems.***

Major Concepts

- ☐ **An opinion is what someone believes is true. A fact is a statement that can be proved to be true.** (page 309)
- ☐ **"Fuzzy thinking" is a catchall phrase that refers to illogical or misleading statements.** (pages 310-311)
- ☐ **Listing and reviewing options are keys to making good decisions.** (page 312)
- ☐ **Brainstorming solutions and using trial and error to test those solutions are helpful tools for solving problems.** (page 313)

Writing as a Learning Tool

(pages 315-317)

Introduction

Students who like to write have already discovered how writing can be used as a tool for learning, whether or not they realize it consciously. Not only is writing important for communicating with others, but it can also help writers figure things out, find and organize their thoughts, and keep in touch with the outside world.

Writing as a Learning Tool showcases three writers—author Toby Fulwiler and his daughters Megan and Anna. Through different examples, each writer shows how to use writing as a learning tool. These real-life examples will awaken your writers to the possibilities of learning from their own writing.

Rationale

- ***It is important to learn how writing can be used for bringing order to thoughts.***
- ***Students need to learn the many ways that writing can be used to improve their learning.***

Major Concepts

- ☐ **Writing is important for communicating with others. It can also help writers figure things out, find and organize their thoughts, and keep in touch with the outside world.** (page 315)
- ☐ **Making a list of ideas on paper can help you organize your thoughts and do something with them.** (page 316)
- ☐ **Writing means connecting with real people for real reasons.** (page 317)

Completing Assignments

(pages 318-321)

Introduction

One of the most difficult adjustments for children in fourth and fifth grades is learning to manage an ever-increasing number of assignments. Many students become frustrated with their teachers' expectations, because they aren't sure how to get the job done. Learning specific techniques for setting goals and managing time can help students gain the confidence they need to meet the challenges of each new grade.

Completing Assignments begins with a "job description" for a student. The next sections describe how to succeed in that all-important job, starting with guidelines for setting goals. Next, helpful hints for effective time management are explained. Finally, a three-step list guides students from the planning stage to the completion of assignments.

Rationale

- ***Many students need to be taught how to set goals.***
- ***Time-management skills help students stay on task.***
- ***When students feel in control of their assignments, their confidence will grow and their work will improve.***

Major Concepts

- ☐ **Setting goals and reaching them is what growing up is all about.** (page 319)
- ☐ **"To Do" lists and weekly schedules are effective time-management tools.** (page 320)
- ☐ **Turning big jobs into little ones makes extended assignments seem less overwhelming and easier to complete.** (page 320)
- ☐ **Proper planning prevents poor performance.** (page 321)

Working in Groups

(pages 322-327)

Introduction

Students enjoy the opportunity to work with their peers, but teachers often find that the work periods degenerate into unproductive gab sessions. Students can learn to work together productively in groups when they master some basic cooperative learning techniques.

Working in Groups begins with a discussion of "people skills." On the next three pages, students learn about making plans, listening to one another, and working cooperatively. In the remaining part of the chapter, guidelines for making decisions, evaluating the group's work, and group sharing are provided.

Rationale

- ***Learning to listen and work together can lead to improved performance in all areas of the curriculum.***
- ***Learning to work cooperatively is an important life skill.***

Major Concepts

- ☐ **Listening, cooperating, and clarifying are important "people skills."** (page 322)
- ☐ **Making a plan can help a group stay on task and complete an assignment.** (page 323)
- ☐ **To listen effectively, students need to think about what is being said.** (page 324)
- ☐ **Cooperating means working with others to reach a shared goal.** (page 325)
- ☐ **Clarifying means "clearing up" confusion in group work.** (page 325)
- ☐ **Group sharing can be used to discuss books that students have read.** (page 327)

Taking Tests

(pages 328-335)

Introduction

Without tests, it wouldn't be school. Tests are an inescapable part of school, but not a pleasant one for most students. Yet tests should be a learning tool, not a torture device!

Taking Tests begins by reassuring students that "tests don't have to be a big deal." Then it explains the two parts of test success: preparing for and taking tests. The following pages provide detailed strategies and techniques (including models) for doing well on both essay and objective tests. Finally, there are several memory-boosting techniques to help students recall material for tests.

Rationale

- ***Learning how to prepare for and take tests gives students a sense of mastery over this sometimes scary (and frustrating) part of school.***
- ***Good test-preparation skills help students reinforce what they have already learned and learn what they missed the first time around.***
- ***When students know how to prepare for and take tests, their performance on tests is a more accurate indicator of what they have learned.***

Major Concepts

- ☐ **Tests help both students and teachers discover what students have learned, and what they haven't.** (page 328)
- ☐ **Test success comes in two stages: *preparing* for the test and *taking* the test.** (page 329)
- ☐ **There are two basic kinds of tests, essay and objective. They require different methods of test preparation and test taking.** (pages 330-333)
- ☐ **Essay tests require students to read, think, organize, and write.** (pages 330-331)
- ☐ **Objective tests may include one or more of the following kinds of questions: true/false, matching, multiple choice, fill in the blanks.** (pages 332-333)
- ☐ **Remembering material is the key to test success, and there are many techniques students can use to improve recall.** (pages 334-335)

Keeping Good Notes

(pages 336-339)

Introduction

Learning how to keep good notes is perhaps the most important skill that students will learn in the fourth and fifth grades. It is one they will use more and more throughout their school years. As students realize how they will need to rely on their notes to prepare for tests, they will want to learn to keep the best notes possible.

Keeping Good Notes begins by discussing the power of writing as a tool for remembering. Guidelines are given for improving note-taking skills. Next, students are introduced to the learning log as a tool. Finally, more learning log activities are described for those who want to branch out in their writing.

Rationale

- ***Being able to take good notes is an important skill, one students will use more and more throughout their school years.***
- ***Learning to write reflectively, as in a learning log, broadens students' school experience, enhancing their understanding of lessons.***

Major Concepts

- ☐ **Writing is a powerful learning tool.** (page 336)
- ☐ **Note taking means listening carefully and writing down just the important ideas.** (page 336)
- ☐ **Three guidelines for improving note-taking skills are pay attention, be brief, and be organized.** (page 337)
- ☐ **Learning logs provide a whole range of possibilities for students to take charge of their own learning.** (pages 338-339)

Handbook Minilessons

Minilessons can transform any classroom into an active learning environment. (We define a minilesson as instruction that lasts about 10-15 minutes and covers a single idea or a core of basic information.) Minilessons can be delivered from the front of the room and include the entire class. They can also be individualized or implemented in writing groups. Ideally, each lesson will address a specific need your students have at a particular time. This makes the lesson meaningful and successful.

In this section, there is one minilesson listed for each chapter in the handbook. You will find this section invaluable when planning activities related to the handbook.

The Process of Writing

Getting Started . . . . *All About Writing*

WRITE about your personal "process" of writing.
ASK yourself: How do I decide on a topic? What do I do next?
COMPARE your process to the one described on **pages 3-5** in your handbook.
Using **pages 6 and 7**, LIST an idea or two that you plan to try for each of the four main steps in the writing process.

Focus Pocus . . . . *One Writer's Process*

GET four index cards. On the first card, LIST words that come to mind when you think about a favorite teacher. On the second card, WRITE a sentence that contains one main idea about this teacher. On the third card, REWRITE your sentence to make it better, using details that show.
RECOPY your sentence in your best handwriting on the fourth card, making sure every word is correct.

Give me an "S." . . . . *A Basic Writing Guide*

READ Shaun McDonnell's words on **page 12** in your handbook. Do you agree? Why or why not? With a partner or your class, DISCUSS how the *Seven Secrets to Success* on **pages 12-15** might help students to enjoy writing.

A Few Favorites . . . . *Planning Your Portfolio*

LIST some of your favorite pieces of writing that you have done in the past.
WRITE a sentence or two about each, explaining why they are your favorites.

Life Map . . . . *Building a File of Writing Ideas*

DRAW your life map. Start with your birth and work right up to the present.
CHOOSE the experiences you want to picture along the way.
SAVE your map in your writing folder to use later for personal writing topics. (See **page 25** in your handbook for a model of a life map.)

Dust Off Your Cluster, Buster! . . . . *Selecting a Subject*

MAKE a cluster for a school-related event.
USE the model on **page 26** in your handbook to get started.
SAVE it in your writing folder for a future writing topic.

The Best (Worst) Place . . . . *Starting Points for Writing*

DESCRIBE the best (or worst) place you have been.
BEGIN your writing with this writing prompt: The first (last) place I want to go back to is . . .
SAVE your writing in your writing folder for future development.

Pencil Talk . . . . *Collecting Details*

MAKE UP a dialogue between two pencils who are talking about all the writing they have to do in your class.
KEEP the conversation going as long as you can without putting your pencil down!
SAVE your imaginary conversation in your writing folder for future use.

Talking Things Through . . . . . . *Planning and Drafting Tips*

TURN to **page 33** and read "Talk About It." Then FIND a partner and TALK about your writing topic.
TAKE notes on any ideas your partner suggests for your topic.
On your own, CHOOSE one of the opening suggestions on the bottom of the page and try writing the first few sentences of your draft.

The Shape of Things to Come . . . . *Writing Forms*

CHOOSE one of the shorter forms of writing on **pages 34 and 35** in your handbook.
EXPERIMENT with one of them.
EXCHANGE your writing with a classmate.
RESPOND to each other's work.

Before and After . . . . *Revising Your Writing*

WRITE a short paragraph about a personal experience. Then decide where you could add "showing" details to the paragraph, using **page 40** in your handbook to help you.
REWRITE your paragraph with your changes. Which one do you like better, the "before" or the "after" paragraph?

Saying the Right Thing .... *Conferencing with Partners*

BRAINSTORM for 5 minutes about all the ways you can help writing partners improve their writing.
ORGANIZE your ideas on paper, using **page 43** in your handbook for additional tips.
FILE the list in your writing folder.
USE your ideas the next time you conference with a partner.

Listen, my son. .... *Sharing Family Stories*

PRETEND that you are a parent.
THINK of an important family story from your life.
SHARE this story in a letter to your "child." Use your handbook chapters on "Sharing Family Stories" and "Writing Friendly Letters" to help you as you write.
GIVE your story a catchy title. Here are some ideas:

I Saved the Day	Grandpa's Fishy Fish Story
Four Aunts in One Kitchen	My Sister's Crazy Plan

Check! .... *Editing and Proofreading*

FIND a short piece of your writing that needs some editing and proofreading.
USE the "Editing and Proofreading Checklist" on **page 53** as a guide.
MAKE your corrections, and WRITE your final copy if there's time.

It's personal. .... *Publishing Your Writing*

USE the instructions on **page 57** in your handbook to help you make a personal writing book (blank book).
DESIGN the cover.
DECIDE whether to use the writing book in school or at home, and SET a regular time to write in your book.

Twins .... *Writing Paragraphs*

READ about Evan on **pages 62-65** in your handbook.
PRETEND Evan has a twin sister.
CHOOSE one of the models as a guide, and WRITE your own paragraph about her.

Rome wasn't built in a day. . . . . *Writing Essays*

WRITE the letters of the alphabet in two columns on a piece of notebook paper, skipping a line between each letter.
LIST one or two possible essay subjects for each letter. (For "a" you might list "assemblies" or "apples." For "b" you might list "brothers" or "bagels.")
WORK on this activity with a classmate if your teacher allows it.
SAVE your writing ideas in your writing folder for future development.

Making Contact . . . . *A Writing Sampler*

PRETEND that aliens have been spotted landing their spaceship on the school roof.
USE the student model on **page 81** in your handbook to help you as you WRITE about this "event."

Combo Challenge . . . . *Writing Basic Sentences*

WRITE two or three short sentences about the illustration on **page 92**. CHALLENGE a partner to combine your sentences, using any of the techniques on **pages 90-93** to make one smoother, detailed sentence.

You've got to please yourself. . . . . *Writing with Style*

READ about developing a sense of style on **page 95** in your handbook. EXPLAIN to a partner what this statement means:

"Writing without details is like baking cookies without flour."

Author! Author! . . . . *Modeling the Masters*

CHOOSE a few lines from a favorite book.
TRY to write your own sentences, following the guidelines for writing on **pages 96-97** in your handbook.
SAVE all your work in your writing folder for future use.

HUNT for answers on **pages 98-101** in your handbook to complete the following definitions. The first one has been done for you.

1. A word that s-t-r-e-t-c-h-e-s the truth is an *exaggeration (page 99)*.
2. Checking a final draft for errors is ____________________.
3. A story from a writer's life is a ____________________.
4. Details that help us to see, feel, smell, taste, and hear a subject are ____________________.
5. Collecting ideas in groups by freely sharing possibilities is ____________________.

The Forms of Writing

A Very Bad-Good Day . . . . *Writing in Journals*

THINK about your best and worst days.
DIVIDE a fresh page in your journal into two columns.
LABEL one "BEST DAY" and the other "WORST DAY." (You may want to draw a smiling face over one column and a frowning face over the other.)
LIST all the things you can remember about each day in the appropriate column.
USE this page to generate a comparison/contrast paragraph in the future.

Who am I? . . . . *Writing Personal Narratives*

BEGIN a collection box for writing topics. (You'll need a shoe box or some other small container.)
PERSONALIZE the box by drawing on it with markers, pasting on pictures and shapes cut from colored paper, and so on. Add to its contents regularly—movie ticket stubs, letters or cards from relatives, photographs, found items, anything that represents you and your life.
PROMISE yourself to keep your collection growing!

Dear Occupant, ...*Writing Friendly Letters*

Have you ever received mail addressed just to you? Have you sent letters to friends or family members recently?
LIST the people you have written to or would like to write to. Keep it general (friend, cousin, grandparent, aunt, and so on).
MAKE a list of all the reasons to write to them. Then TURN to **page 116** of your handbook. Did you list any of the reasons you find there?

For the Record . . . .*Writing Newspaper Stories*

Using the tips for interviewing on **page 125** of your handbook, PREPARE a list of questions to ask someone that you find interesting.
If possible, INTERVIEW that person and PUBLISH your interview (with permission) in the school paper or newsletter.

A bird in the hand is worth . . . . *Writing Book Reviews*

RECALL a favorite folktale or fable. REFLECT on the following questions:

1. What do you think the author wants you to learn from the story?
2. What happens in the story that leads you to believe this is the author's message?

SHARE your review of the story with your classmates.

★ ● ■ . . . . *Writing Explanations*

DRAW a picture of a simple shape.
Without naming the shape, WRITE an explanation of how to draw it.
EXCHANGE papers with a partner. (Keep the drawing hidden from view until after your partner has tried to draw the shape.) If your explanation is clear, your drawings will be similar.

"For Matt" . . . . *Writing Business Letters*

MAKE a handy pattern for the business-letter form. Use your own paper or put it on computer. Follow the format on **page 145** in your handbook.
LABEL the parts of a business letter clearly, leaving room for the information. Provide three lines for the heading, skip three to six lines, provide four lines for the inside address, and so on.
SAVE the pattern for future use.

Recess rocks! . . . . *Writing Observation Reports*

TAKE your notebook with you when you go outside for recess.
RECORD all of the sights, sounds, smells, and physical sensations you notice for 10 minutes.
WRITE a short report that includes the sensory data you collected.
READ your recess report to your class.

Shooting Star . . . . *Writing Fantasies*

Using your favorite colored pencil or pen, WRITE your favorite wish in the middle of a blank sheet of paper. Then surround the wish with ideas about everything that would happen if the wish came true.
USE your cluster to write a fantasy based on your wish.

He lassoed Texas! . . . . *Writing Tall Tales*

SEARCH your favorite tall tale for examples of sentences that exaggerate. (See **page 163** in your handbook for a list of stories to read and choose from.)
SHARE the sentences in class.
DISCUSS why they are good examples of exaggeration.

Deposit another quarter. . . . . *Writing Realistic Stories*

Work with a partner to CREATE an imaginary phone conversation between two of your favorite cartoon characters.
MAKE this conversation sound as realistic as possible.
PERFORM it for your classmates.

"Wait for me, Magellan." . . . . . *Writing Stories from History*

PRETEND that you are packing for a trip around the world with Magellan. (See **page 172** in your handbook.)
MAKE a list of all the things you would take along to help you survive. Then CROSS out any item on your list that would not have been available in Magellan's day. What are you left with?

Color me glad. . . . . *Writing Poems*

READ "Purple Poems" on **page 179** of your handbook.
WRITE a color poem of your own.
SAVE it in your writing folder.

Ole Nan Needle! . . . . *Writing Songs*

FIND some others words to use for the underlined words in the following line from a song: My Aunt Nan can scare a gnat.
USE a dictionary, a thesaurus, and your own imagination! Here is an example:

Ole Nan Needle can startle a beetle.

REVISE the line again, using words that have similar sounds. Does your line make a good start for a song?
SAVE it in your writing folder for a rainy day.

Exit, stage right! . . . . *Writing Plays*

BECOME a playwright! All you need to get started is at least two characters, a problem, and a place or a setting for the action.
USE the collection sheet on **page 194** in your handbook to help you get started.
SAVE your ideas in your writing folder for future development.

What's black and white and re(a)d all over? . . . *Writing Riddles*

LOOK at the "Crack Up" riddles on **page 199**. They use words that sound alike, and are sometimes even spelled alike, but have different meanings.
EXPLAIN the meaning of each word in the pairs below.
USE a dictionary to help you.

1. star/star ______________________________
2. pain/pane ______________________________
3. knight/night ______________________________
4. aisle/isle ______________________________
5. brush/brush ______________________________
6. beau/bow ______________________________
7. dough/dough ______________________________

Special Challenge: WRITE a riddle using one or more of the word pairs above.

Say it with pictures. . . . . *Writing for Fun*

MAKE a storyboard, using the model on **page 204** of your handbook. (If you're stuck for a story idea, CHECK your writing folder or idea box for writing topics. Also see the suggestions on **page 29** of your handbook.)
With your teacher's permission, MOUNT the finished storyboard on tagboard or stiff paper and DISPLAY it in the classroom

Book Worm . . . . *Using the Library*

DRAW a simple map of your library.
INCLUDE these items: the spot where you can usually find the librarian, card catalog (or computer-catalog terminals), checkout desk, biographies, novels, nonfiction books, reference books, new books, and magazines.
SHOW your work to your teacher and librarian.

In summary . . . . *Writing a Summary*

SELECT a short news article from a newspaper or magazine. MASK its title. Then EXCHANGE articles with a partner. Ask the "Big Questions" on **page 219** in your handbook to help you decide on the main idea.
WRITE a title for the article and compare it to the actual one. Did you find the main idea?

Nitty "Griddy" . . . . *Writing a Classroom Report*

GET STARTED on writing a report. MAKE a gathering grid for any topic you find interesting. (Use the grid example on **page 226** in your handbook.)
INCLUDE questions that you would like answered.
KEEP the grid handy, and FILL in the grid as you learn more about your topic.

The Tools of Learning

SRN . . . . *Using Reading Strategies*

GRAB any textbook you have.
TURN to a chapter you haven't read yet.
REVIEW **page 240** in your handbook for an explanation and example of SRN (Survey, Read, Note). Then USE the strategy for the chapter you turned to.

Feelings . . . . *Using Reading Strategies*

ANSWER these questions in your reading journal for the last book you read on your own.

1. What were your feelings after reading the opening chapter(s) of this book?
2. After reading half of the book?
3. After finishing the book?

KEEP these "before, during, and after" questions handy while reading your next book. You may want to share your responses with a reading partner or group.

A picture is worth . . . . *Reading Pictures*

INVENT new symbols for the top three signs on **page 247** in your handbook.
USE your imagination! TRY out your new symbols on several friends. Did they understand your messages?

People say "BRrrr" in FeBRuary. . . *Becoming a Better Speller*

INVENT sayings to help you and your classmates remember how to spell the months of the year.
MAKE up sayings for four or five of the months you find the hardest to spell. (See the spelling list on **pages 358-361** and the memory techniques on **page 334** for help.)
POST each saying near the calendar in your classroom for the appropriate month.
Here's an example: JaNUary is NUmber one with me!

They're related. . . . . *Building Vocabulary Skills*

SUBSTITUTE better words for the "lazy" words that are underlined in each sentence below. (Check out **page 257** in your handbook for information about finding the right word.)

1. The old car's old tires needed repair.

1. ______________________________

____

2. As soon as the bicyclist goes by, the squirrel will run across the road.

2. ______________________________

____

3. Elsie walks two miles to the big grocery store every Saturday.

3. ______________________________

____

Now WRITE sentences with "lazy" words of your own and ASK a partner to revise them.

Bravo! . . . . *Giving Speeches*

CHOOSE a story you really like and can tell in 2-3 minutes.
WRITE down each thing that happens in the story, using a different note card for each event. PUT the cards in order and MEMORIZE them all.
PRACTICE telling the story until you don't need the note cards anymore.
TELL the story to your group or class.

Mime Time . . . . *Performing Poems*

FIND a short poem that "shows" a lot of action.
ASK a partner to read the poem while you PANTOMIME the action lines.
PRACTICE the poem until the timing is perfect.
PERFORM it for an audience.

5 W's and H . . . . *Improving Viewing Skills*

CHOOSE a television news program and WATCH at least one complete story.
While watching, TAKE a few notes on the story, using the 5 W's and H on **page 290** in your handbook.
REPORT the story to your class. (You and your classmates could plan a regular news "hour" of your own.)

Telephone . . . . *Improving Listening Skills*

PLAY the game "telephone" with your group or class.
BEGIN by giving the directions for getting from your bedroom to the refrigerator, or any other object in your house.
WHISPER them to the next person "on the line." The last person in the game should repeat your directions aloud. Are they accurate? If not, review the "Good Listener Checklist" on **page 293** in your handbook, and TRY again.

Getting It Together . . . . *Getting Organized*

USE the "Ask Questions" graphic organizer on **page 296** in your handbook to organize information about a class party or school event.
Then WRITE a sample invitation.

First-Letter Fun . . . . *Thinking and Writing*

CREATE a memory device, using the first letter of each of the guidelines for thinking and writing on **page 307** in your handbook. Here's an example:

Randy Utters "Ahem!" Anytime Squeak Escapes.

Now WRITE your own silly sentence to help you remember the categories.
REFER to this page whenever your thinking and writing assignments involve key words like "describe" or "compare."

Just the facts, ma'am. . . . . *Thinking and Writing*

LIST the things you know about a favorite wild animal.
Then LOOK UP your topic in several reference books.
PLACE a check mark in front of the factual statements in your list.
USE these facts to write a paragraph about your topic, using **page 302** in your handbook to help you organize your paragraph.

I can work it out. *Thinking Clearly*

THINK about a big problem you need to solve or have recently solved.
CONSIDER the guidelines on **page 313** in your handbook and answer the questions in your journal.
SAVE the page for a handy reference whenever you face a new problem.

Goal to Go . . . . *Completing Assignments*

IDENTIFY three goals you would like to reach by the end of this school year.
In your journal, WRITE each goal on a separate page. As you work toward your goals, RECORD the steps you took to accomplish them.
GIVE yourself a reward when you reach a goal, and TELL at least one other person about it.

Sticking to My Schedule . . . . *Completing Assignments*

USE **page 320** in your handbook to make a Weekly Planner for yourself, or use a printed form.
CHALLENGE yourself to stick with it.
DO the "Think About It" on this page to help you plan your work time better.
At the end of the week, EVALUATE your planner. Did it help you get assignments in on time? Why or why not?

Goin' West . . . . *Working in Groups*

FORM a small group (three to five students) and PRETEND that you are part of a wagon train that is heading west to California in 1848. Winter has come early, and your group must decide whether to stop where you are, or keep moving. (You may add any details you want to make this scenario more "real." Perhaps the food supply is running low, or one of the horses is limping.)
REACH a consensus on what to do, using the guidelines on **page 326** in your handbook to help form a plan.

Did you say "test"? . . . . *Taking Tests*

After reading about the essay test on **pages 330-331** in your handbook, WRITE an essay-test question and its answer for a science topic that you are studying now.
SHARE it with your study group or class.

Learning As I Go . . . . *.Keeping Good Notes*

KEEP a "learning log" for a week. (You may use several pages of your journal or notebook.)
Using the activities on **pages 338-339** in your handbook, RECORD your reactions to each of your classes. What did you do? What did you learn? What ideas do you have for doing tomorrow's assignments?
At the end of the week, EVALUATE the log's usefulness. Did it help you keep track of your learning?

Proofreader's Guide: Check It Out

Short Change . . . . *Marking Punctuation (4)*

LIST three different ways periods are used in the following sentences besides as the end punctuation of each sentence (topic number 01). Then CHECK your handbook **(pages 343-344)** to see how you did.

1. I might as well change my name to I. M. Short.
2. I only have $4.93, and I owe my neighbor $5.75.
3. When I tell her my problem, I'm sure that Ms. Jackson will not be very happy.

1. ______________________________

2. ______________________________

3. ______________________________

Charlie's Horse . . . . *Marking Punctuation (5)*

LIST the names of seven people you know. Next to each name, WRITE its possessive form. (Hint: You'll need seven apostrophes. See your handbook, **page 349**, topic number 45, for details!)

1. ______________ ______________

2. ______________ ______________

3. ______________ ______________

4. ______________ ______________

5. ______________ ______________

6. ______________ ______________

7. ______________ ______________

Give me an example. . . . . *Editing for Mechanics (4)*

Pages 352-354 of your handbook list the rules for capitalization. The rules are found under topic numbers 63-76. FIND each of the topic numbers listed below. READ each rule. Then, on the line next to each topic number, WRITE one example of a word or phrase that is capitalized according to the rule. Do not write a word that is shown in your handbook. The first example has been done for you. THINK of the rest on your own!

65. Grandpa ______ 74. ______

67. ______ 75. ______

72. ______ 76. ______

Taking Shortcuts . . . . *Editing for Mechanics (4)*

MATCH each of the following abbreviations to the word or phrase it represents. See **pages 356** and **357** in your handbook for help.

____ 1.	Mr.	a. et cetera (and so forth)
____ 2.	Mrs.	b. as soon as possible
____ 3.	Ms.	c. kilogram
____ 4.	etc.	d. post meridiem (after noon)
____ 5.	a.m.	e. combination of Miss and Missus
____ 6.	p.m.	f. Missus
____ 7.	ASAP	g. ante meridiem (before noon)
____ 8.	kg	h. Mister

To Cap or Not to Cap . . . . *Editing for Mechanics (5)*

The following words are sometimes capitalized. It depends on how the word is used in the sentence. (See handbook **pages 352-354**.)

WRITE two sentences using each word: one sentence in which the word is capitalized, and one in which it is not. (*One more thing:* Do not use the words as first words in your sentences!)

mother	north	white house
president	earth	war

Puppies on the Loose . . . . *Editing for Mechanics (5)*

IMAGINE that your dog has six puppies. One day while you're at school, the puppies romp through the house, destroying everything in sight.

WRITE a short story about the puppies' day, using the plural forms of as many of the following words as you can. (See handbook **page 355**.)

shoe	dish	tomato	guppy
sofa	box	turkey	paw
pillow	candy	loaf	nose

Don't MTB; it's PN! . . . . *Editing for Mechanics (5)*

Think of at least five phrases that you use all the time—"no way," "pizza night," "home before dark," "miss the bus," etc.

TURN all your phrases into initialisms. (Into what? Check your handbook, **page 356**, topic number 91.)

For Example: "miss the bus" becomes MTB; "pizza night" becomes PN.

Now WRITE a paragraph using all your initialisms.

TRADE paragraphs with a partner.

FIGURE OUT each other's initialisms. What do they stand for?

"C" Snakes . . . . *Check Your Spelling (4)*

Certain words appear in the list of commonly misspelled words on **pages 358-361** in your handbook because they have letters that are pronounced like other letters. "Certain" is one of those words. The "c" makes the sound of "s." It sounds like the word should be spelled "sertain."

LIST at least 10 other words in which a "c" makes the "s" sound on **pages 358-361** in your handbook. The first word has been listed for you.

1. accept
2. __________
3. __________
4. __________
5. __________
6. __________
7. __________
8. __________
9. __________
10. __________

Short, but Not Always Simple . . . . . *Check Your Spelling (5)*

Just because a word is short does not mean it is easy to spell. There may be a letter that you do not hear when you pronounce the word, or a sound that could be spelled several different ways.

LOOK for 10 three- or four-letter words in the list of commonly misspelled words on **pages 358-361** in your handbook. CHOOSE ones that cause you trouble, and write them down.

TALK about why each one might be easy to misspell.

WRITE a brief paragraph that uses as many of these short words as possible. UNDERLINE each short word that you used from your list.

ASK a partner to read your paragraph and check the spellings of your underlined words, using the list of commonly misspelled words.

On the Board . . . . *Using the Right Word (4)*

FILL IN the blanks in the sentences below, using "a" or "an," whichever is correct. Check **page 362** in your handbook for help.

1. Our classroom has ________ bulletin board.
2. There is ________ calendar on the board.
3. Once ________ month, we put new pictures on the board.
4. Right now, there are pictures of ________ eagle, ________ owl, and ________ parrot on the board.
5. Paula has ________ idea for next month's board.
6. She wants to put up pictures of ________ astronaut.

Who's on first? . . . . *Using the Right Word (5)*

FILL IN the blanks in the sentences below, using "whose" or "who's," whichever is correct. Check **page 369** in your handbook for help.

1. ___________ book is this?
2. It belongs to Jordan, ___________ in my math class.
3. ___________ going to the recycling center?
4. ___________ turn is it to go?
5. This is Sanjeev, ___________ family is from India.
6. Is he the one ___________ new here?
7. ___________ science class are you in?
8. My teacher is Ms. Chang, ___________ from China.

The pig crashed into the cow. . . *Understanding Sentences (4)*

WRITE three run-on sentences that are all about things running into each other. (**Example:** My dad backed our car into our neighbor's car the two cars locked bumpers.)

EXCHANGE your run-on sentences and CORRECT them. If you need help, see **page 87** in your handbook.

And Then I Said . . . . *Understanding Sentences (4)*

WRITE a rambling sentence about how you spent one day. It could be a day at school, at an amusement park, or anywhere. (**Page 87** in your handbook gives an example of a rambling sentence.) Include what you did, what you ate, how you felt, and so on. When you're done, go back and CORRECT your rambling sentence. Make your new sentences as smooth and as fun to read as possible.

The Four Seasons . . . . *Understanding Sentences (4)*

WRITE an acrostic (name) poem for one of the four seasons—winter, spring, summer, autumn. USE only adjectives. See **page 384** in your handbook for more about adjectives; see "Name Poetry" on **page 187** for more about an acrostic poem.

Example:

WINTER
White
Icy
Nasty
Terrific
Endless
Radiant

Then CREATE a four-seasons bulletin board, decorated with original artwork.

Special Challenge: THINK of other themes for writing acrostic poems—the four directions on the compass, the colors of the rainbow, and so on. Consider themes that would make dramatic bulletin boards for sharing your poems.

Says who? . . . . *Understanding Sentences (5)*

Although sentence fragments are errors in your writing (see your handbook, **page 87**), they're okay in your talking! People use fragments all the time when they talk to each other:

"Going to the mall?"

"No money."

"Basketball?"

"Too cold."

WRITE a short conversation between two people. Make everything they say a fragment.

Then REWRITE each piece of dialogue as a complete sentence.

And so on, and so on . . . . . . *Understanding Sentences (5)*

FIND a very short news article (two or three paragraphs) in a newspaper. COPY the article onto a sheet of paper, leaving out all the end punctuation and initial capital letters. Add the word "and" in each place where a sentence ended. In other words, make the article into one long, rambling sentence.

Now TRADE papers with a classmate who has done the same thing. CORRECT each other's rambling sentences. If you need help, see **page 87** in your handbook.

Finally, COMPARE your corrected sentences with the original article. Your sentences don't have to match the article exactly, as long as they are correct and the meaning is clear.

Find Festus! . . . . *Understanding Our Language (4)*

READ about prepositions and prepositional phrases on **page 386** in your handbook. Then TURN to **page 111** in your handbook and READ "The Great Gerbil Escape." FIND and WRITE down the prepositional phrases from the first four paragraphs in this story.

LABEL the part of speech of each object of the preposition in your phrases. The first one has been done for you.

Paragraph 1: of gerbils (noun), from our bathtub ______

Paragraph 2: ______

Paragraph 3: ______

Paragraph 4: ______

______

They agree! . . . . *Understanding Our Language (4)*

STUDY "Agreement of Pronouns" on the top of **page 378** in your handbook. Notice that the word "antecedent" refers to the noun that the pronoun replaces. Antecedent means "comes before." A pronoun must *always* have a noun that comes before it.

SPEND several minutes writing a list of interesting nouns. SELECT your favorite noun from the list. Then WRITE a sentence using that noun and also a pronoun that refers back to it.

SHARE your sentence with the class. Decide whether the pronouns in each sentence agree with the nouns they replace.

Points of View . . . . *Understanding Our Language (4)*

STUDY the section "Person of a Pronoun" on **page 378** in your handbook. Then, on **page 82**, find and read the story "I'm Growing Up."

Working with a partner, have one person READ the selection, changing all the *first-person* references to *second-person* pronouns. (Make the changes as you read out loud, but quietly, to your partner.) Then have the other person READ the same selection, changing all the *first-person* references to *third-person* pronouns.

DISCUSS the effect of changing the point of view in reading or writing a story. SHARE your findings with a classmate.

What am I? . . . . *Understanding Our Language (5)*

COMPOSE a "What Am I" riddle about 2-3 objects in your classroom.

Example: *I have a mouth and silver teeth that fall out everywhere. What am I? (answer: Stapler)*

SHARE your riddle with a classmate and listen to his or hers.

LIST all the riddle answers on the lines below. SEE handbook **page 375** for an explanation of abstract and concrete nouns. LABEL each noun "abstract" or "concrete." What have you discovered?

stapler	*concrete*

Name Dropper . . . . *Understanding Our Language (5)*

REVIEW the list of irregular verbs in your handbook on **page 382**.

FIND two irregular verbs that begin with the first letter in your first or last name. (If that doesn't work, use the name of a friend or family member.)

WRITE three crazy sentences for each verb by completing the sentence starters below. (Make sure that you use the correct form of the verb.)

1. *Yesterday, I* ______________________

2. *I have* ______________________

3. *I will* ______________________

The Student Almanac

Give me a sign. . . . . *Useful Tables and Lists (4)*

The sign language shown on **page 391** in your handbook has a sign for each letter of the alphabet. Other sign languages have a sign for each word. (Some Native Americans held up two fingers to sign "friend," and put their hand to their mouth to sign "water.")

Working in groups, CREATE your own sign language. Imagine that you've been shipwrecked on an island, and the people there don't speak English. How could you sign that your ship sank? That you're hungry? What else would you need to say?

The Nanny Said to the Kid, *"Ba-a-a!"* *Useful Tables and Lists (4)*

LOOK at the table of animal facts on **page 393** in your handbook. CHOOSE one of the animals listed in the table.

WRITE a paragraph about that animal, using all the terms for it shown in the chart. Your paragraph may be fact or fantasy!

Hand Signals . . . . *Useful Tables and Lists (5)*

LOOK at the sign language chart on **page 391** in your handbook. In order to use this sign language well, you have to learn and practice it. Then you can only "talk" to someone else who has also learned it.

As a class, THINK of as many hand signals as you can that everybody already knows, such as the one for "stop." If you play (or watch) sports, show the hand signals used in the games.

Finally, CHOOSE a password, and have everybody in the class learn to sign it, using the sign language shown in your handbook.

Great Gaggles of Geese! . . . . . . *Useful Tables and Lists (5)*

LOOK at the table of animal facts on **page 393** in your handbook.

WRITE a short story about either farm animals or jungle animals. Choose from the animals listed in the table, and use as many of the words from the table as you can.

In Orbit . . . . *Useful Tables and Lists (5)*

Look at "Planet Profiles" on **page 398** and the chart on **page 399** in your handbook.

WRITE a simple question that could be answered easily by finding information in one box on the chart.

WRITE a slightly harder question that requires comparing two or more planets.

Finally, WRITE a question for which you must compare all the planets.

SHARE your questions with the entire class.

Times are changing. . . . . *Improving Math Skills (4)*

Jon bought a notebook for $1.89, three pencils for $.49 each, a ruler for $.97, and a ballpoint pen for $2.69. He gave the clerk $10.

SOLVE this problem. How much change did he get back? (SEE **pages 418-419** in your handbook for help.) Show your work.

Now WRITE your own word problem, similar to the one above. CHANGE the objects and the prices. A few volunteers may put their problems on the board for discussion.

When Letters Are Numbers . . . . . *Improving Math Skills (4)*

Roman numerals are letters that stand for numbers. TURN to **page 421** of your handbook, and LOOK at the table of Roman numerals at the bottom.

Using the table, FILL IN the blanks below with the number that each Roman numeral represents.

1. I = ____________ 3. X = ____________ 5. C = ____________

2. V = ____________ 4. L = ____________ 6. M = ____________

The clock strikes twelve. . . . . . . *Improving Math Skills (5)*

SOLVE the following word problem, using the five steps explained on **page 418** in your handbook.

A cuckoo clock has a cuckoo bird that comes out of its birdhouse and cuckoos each hour: once at one o'clock, twice at two o'clock, three times at three o'clock, and so on. How many times does the cuckoo bird cuckoo in one whole day?

It all adds up. . . . . *Improving Math Skills (5)*

READ **pages 418-419** in your handbook and solve this problem: How many runs did the Wildcats score if they scored three runs in each of the first three innings and three runs in each of the last two innings of their baseball game?

SOLVE this problem by using addition. (Show your work.)

Then SOLVE the same problem using multiplication. (Show your work.)

CREATE a problem that could be solved by addition or multiplication. Try to base the problem on your own experience.

EXCHANGE problems with a classmate and write out the solutions.

Know your rights. . . . . *History in the Making (4)*

READ **page 426** in your handbook, "The Bill of Rights." CHOOSE one of the amendments that you think is very important, and WRITE a paragraph stating why you feel this is an important right for people to have.

For help writing your paragraph, read **page 64** in your handbook. It explains persuasive paragraphs.

Your Life Span . . . . *History in the Making (4)*

FIND the "Historical Time Line" in your handbook on **pages 430-439**.
FIND the years during which you have lived. How many years is that?
During which other period in history (of that many years) on the time line would you like to have lived?
SHARE your thinking with the class.
Special Challenge: Use your ideas as the start of a short historical fiction story.

Taking Their Time . . . . *History in the Making (4)*

Using the "Historical Time Line" in your handbook on **pages 430-439**, FIND OUT when a parent, grandparent, or other relative was born.
DECIDE which events, discoveries, inventions, and so on, in that person's lifetime are the most interesting to you.
Talk to this family member about his or her own memories of the event, discovery, or other happening. SHARE the results of your research with your classmates.

Long, Long Ago . . . . *History in the Making (5)*

Open your handbook to **pages 430-435**. Working in small groups, CHOOSE one of the following centuries:

1500's 1600's 1700's 1800's

DISCUSS how one event from the century you chose has affected (and may still be affecting) people's lives.
SHARE what you discover with the entire class. You could make your presentation in the form of a song, poem, newscast, story, skit, and so on.

Inventing Stories . . . . *History in the Making (5)*

TURN to the historical time line that begins on **page 430** in your handbook.
CHOOSE any invention listed in the Science and Inventions section.
WRITE a short fantasy story (it can be one paragraph or more) about how the invention could have come about. Use the handbook chapter "Writing Fantasies" to help you. Finally, CHECK an encyclopedia to find out the real story behind your invention!

Handbook Minilessons Answer Key

Provided in this section is an answer key for the few minilessons requiring specific answers. In most cases, the students' answers for the minilessons will vary.

The Process of Writing

Coming to Terms . . . . *Writing Terms*

1. A word that s-t-r-e-t-c-h-e-s the truth is an *exaggeration (page 99)*
2. Checking a final draft for errors is *proofreading (page 101)*
3. A story from a writer's life is a *personal narrative (page 100)*
4. Details that help us to see, feel, smell, taste, and hear a subject are

   sensory details (page 101)
5. Collecting ideas in groups by freely sharing possibilities is

   brainstorming (page 98)

Proofreader's Guide: Check It Out

Short Change . . . . *Marking Punctuation (4)*

1. *I.M.—after an initial (topic number 03)*
2. *$4.93, $5.75—as a decimal (topic number 04)*
3. *Ms.—after abbreviations (topic number 05)*

Taking Shortcuts . . . . *Editing for Mechanics (4)*

h	1. Mr.	a. et cetera (and so forth)
f	2. Mrs.	b. as soon as possible
e	3. Ms.	c. kilogram
a	4. etc.	d. post meridiem (after noon)
g	5. a.m.	e. combination of Miss and Missus
d	6. p.m.	f. Missus
b	7. ASAP	g. ante meridiem (before noon)
c	8. kg	h. Mister

Puppies on the Loose . . . . *Editing for Mechanics (5)*

shoe *shoes*	dish *dishes*	tomato *tomatoes*	guppy *guppies*
sofa *sofas*	box *boxes*	turkey *turkeys*	paw *paws*
pillow *pillows*	candy *candies*	loaf *loaves*	nose *nose*

"C" Snakes . . . . *.Check Your Spelling (4)*

1. *accept*	6. *bicycle*
2. *accident*	7. *celebration*
3. *century*	8. *cemetary*
4. *city*	9. *patience*
5. *audience*	10. *(Answers will vary.)*

On the Board . . . . *Using the Right Word (4)*

1. Our classroom has ___a___ bulletin board.
2. There is ___a___ calendar on the board.
3. Once ___a___ month, we put new pictures on the board.
4. Right now, there are pictures of ___an___ eagle, ___an___ owl, and ___a___ parrot on the board.
5. Paula has ___an___ idea for next month's board.
6. She wants to put up pictures of ___an___ astronaut.

Who's on first? . . . . *Using the Right Word (5)*

1. ___Whose___ book is this?
2. It belongs to Jordan, ___who's___ in my math class.
3. ___Who's___ going to the recycling center?
4. ___Whose___ turn is it to go?
5. This is Sanjeev, ___whose___ family is from India.
6. Is he the one ___who's___ new here?
7. ___Whose___ science class are you in?
8. My teacher is Ms. Chang, ___who's___ from China.

Find Festus! . . . . *Understanding Our Language (4)*

Paragraph 1: of gerbils (noun), from our bathtub (noun)

Paragraph 2: in your tub (noun), in toys (noun) and sunflower seeds (noun)

Paragraph 3: over the edge (noun), of the tub (noun)

Paragraph 4: down the heat vent (noun), in the wall (noun), beside the vent (noun), into the vent (noun), in a towel (noun)

The Student Almanac

Times are changing. . . . . *Improving Math Skills (4)*

$ .49
× 3
$ 1.47

$ 1.89
.97
2.69
+ 1.47
$ 7.02

$ 10.00
− 7.02
$ 2.98

When Letters Are Numbers . . . . . *Improving Math Skills (4)*

1. I = 1
2. V = 5
3. X = 10
4. L = 50
5. C = 100
6. M = 1,000

The clock strikes twelve. . . . . . . *Improving Math Skills (5)*

156 times

It all adds up. . . . . *Improving Math Skills (5)*

ADDITION

$$\begin{array}{r}1\\1\\+\,1\\\hline 3\end{array}\qquad\begin{array}{r}1\\1\\+\,1\\\hline 3\end{array}\qquad\begin{array}{r}1\\1\\+\,1\\\hline 3\end{array}\qquad\begin{array}{r}3\\+\,3\\\hline 6\end{array}\qquad\begin{array}{r}3\\3\\3\\+\,6\\\hline 15\end{array}$$

MULTIPLICATION

$$\begin{array}{r}3\\\times\,3\\\hline 9\end{array}\qquad\begin{array}{r}3\\\times\,2\\\hline 6\end{array}\qquad\begin{array}{r}6\\+\,9\\\hline 15\end{array}$$

Evaluating/ Assessing/ Monitoring

The information in this section will help you evaluate your students' language and learning progress. Included are general evaluating guidelines; specific strategies for evaluating basic skills, extended units, and writing; and evaluating and responding masters that you can use with your students.

Evaluating Your Students' Work

An effective language and learning program must have at its core a clear, consistent, and pedagogically sound approach to evaluation. The ultimate goal of evaluation should be to help students improve their overall language proficiency. The guidelines and strategies that follow have been designed with these important points in mind.

Special Note: To help students become active participants in the evaluation process, make sure that they know how to use *Writers Express*. It's especially important that they become familiar with The "Process of Writing" section.

How should I evaluate my students' work?

The best methods of evaluation are those that are consistent with the principles of whole language instruction. Evaluation should be

- holistic in nature (assessing a learner's overall performance)
- interesting and functional in design
- open-ended and flexible in scope
- meaningful and relevant to the learner

How can I assess my students' overall performance?

You should generally employ three methods of evaluation: observation, interaction, and analysis.

- When you *observe* a student at work, make note of the student's enthusiasm, diligence, care, creativity, neatness, and so on.
- When you *interact* with a student, informally question the student about his or her work in progress. Also engage in small-group discussions and conduct student/teacher conferences.
- When you *analyze* a student's work, determine what the student already knows about language and how the student is developing as a language learner.

Should I employ all three of these methods of evaluation each time my students work on an activity?

No, it would be next to impossible to observe and interact with students as well as analyze their work for each and every language activity. However, we do suggest that you make use of all three methods of assessment through the course of the school year.

For example, let's say you ask your students to complete 3-5 minutes free writing. You might observe and make note of each student's ability to write for a sustained length of time.

For another activity, you might ask students some basic questions about their work in progress and make note of their responses.

For still another activity, you might carefully analyze the students' finished products. That is, you might highlight particular strengths in their work, suggest how they might do something differently next time, make note of your overall impressions, and award the work a predetermined point total, mark, or comment.

Note: Make sure your students know how their work will be evaluated before they begin. Better yet, let them help you determine how their work will be evaluated.

Should I do all of the evaluating?

No, evaluation should be part of the learning process and should involve students as much as possible. Students automatically become involved in the process if they complete self-evaluation sheets or briefly reflect on their learning progress in a notebook or journal. Questions that students might ask of themselves include the following: Did things go as I planned in this activity? What did I like the best about my work? What caused me the most problems? What could I do to improve my performance the next time we do this type of activity? And so on.

Students can also participate in peer-evaluation conferences or peer-response groups. These conferences work best if students have a predetermined critique sheet (set of general characteristics) with which to judge their peers' work. Don't expect students to be careful, insightful, and fair evaluators right from the start. This will only come through guided practice. (The *Writers Express* student handbook contains information on conferencing with partners and working in groups.)

How do I keep track of all of this evaluating?

Good question. When you evaluate student work holistically, managing all the different elements does become an important issue. We suggest that you have students keep a folder for all their work, including peer- or self-evaluation sheets. Ask them to keep all their drafts for writing projects together, all their language activities and class notes together, and so on.

Should I assign a grade or mark for each activity?

We certainly don't recommend it. You don't have the time to review each activity carefully enough to assign a grade. On top of that, grading each activity is not a very productive method of evaluating. Grades generally get in the way of learning because they represent a stopping point, an end result. A more open-ended system of evaluation is much more in line with the current thinking on assessment.

We believe a basic "performance" score is sufficient for most of the activities. All you have to do is assign students a predetermined number of points (5), a comment (Excellent), or mark (+) upon completion of their work. (The score they receive depends on their basic performance.) We also believe teachers should make at least one specific, positive comment on individual activity sheets whenever possible.

How do I evaluate the students' work at the end of the quarter or semester?

If you have students keep a folder of their work and evaluations, you have a complete file for each student to review. If you noted observations and interactions during various activities, you have your own personal comments and reactions to consider. If you and your students have done both, then you have more than enough material to assess each student's performance.

Make sure your criteria for grading reflects each student's progress as a language learner as much as (or more than) it reflects end products.

How do I address basic-skills competency?

It has been proved in study after study that learning the "basic skills" (grammar and punctuation) out of context has little relevance for young learners and little carryover when they are involved in meaningful language experiences. Students learn about their language when they put language to good use. That is, they learn about their language when they thoughtfully write, read, speak, listen, and think.

When you notice that a student has difficulty using a punctuation mark or a particular verb form, help him or her deal with this problem. There's little incentive to learn if you penalize students for making particular errors in an individual piece of writing. There's all the incentive in the world to learn if you reward them for attempting to correct the error over the long term.

Helping Each Student: Let's say one of your student writers regularly misuses commas. You can do a number of things to help the student address this problem:

- First, note the problem. Don't make a big issue of it. Simply make it clear to the student what the problem is and why it is a problem.
- Then refer the student to the handbook so he or she can see how to correct the problem.
- Also have the student keep track of this error in a special section of the notebook so he or she will know what to look for the next time a piece of writing must be edited and proofread.
- If you feel the problem demands special attention or it is a problem common to many students in the class, consider assigning a related minilesson, or create a series of minilessons to address the problem. (See page 91-120 in this guide for sample minilessons.)

Let students know that you expect them to watch for the problem in future writing assignments. Then when you evaluate their work at the end of the term, check to see what progress they are making.

How do I evaluate extended units?

You have the opportunity with extended units to put all the methods of holistic evaluation into practice. That is, there is enough time during a particular unit to observe students in action, to talk to them about their work, and to analyze the results of their efforts. All it takes on your part is some planning. You decide which aspects of the unit lend themselves best to the different methods of evaluation.

In *The Whole Language Evaluation Book,* Karen Sabers Dalrymple discusses an evaluation format that she finds effective for extended units. She focuses her evaluation on three different stages of the students' work—referred to as the perceiving, ideating, and presenting stages. The *perceiving* stage focuses on the introductory material presented during a unit. Opening discussions and getting-started activities are "perceiving" activities. You should observe and note how students react and contribute to the opening material.

The *ideating* stage focuses on how students carry out the assigned work. You will again want to observe and note the students' efforts during this stage. You will also want to talk to students about their work and, perhaps, informally analyze their work in progress.

The *presenting* stage focuses on the finished products students share. During this final stage, you will want to observe and assess any oral presentations and carefully analyze finished projects. (Use the observation/assessment sheet provided on page 137 to help you keep track of your students' progress during extended units.)

How should I evaluate writing?

As you know, a great deal has been "written" about the teaching of writing, including how to evaluate writing as a process rather than an end product. We have encapsulated much of this information starting on page 139 of this section. Insights into assessing writing in progress (formative evaluation) as well as insights into assessing the end results of writing (summative evaluation) are addressed here.

Recently, much attention has been given to special writing portfolios in which students compile their best written work for evaluation at the end of a term. Portfolios place a significant part of the assessment process in the hands of the student writers because they can pick and choose what they want evaluated. Students appreciate the sense of ownership this gives them. Teachers appreciate portfolio writing because it reduces the number of finished papers they have to assess, and the papers they do read are the students' best efforts. (Guidelines for using writing portfolios are included in this section of your teacher's guide starting on page 143. There is also a section on portfolios in the *Writers Express* student handbook, pages 18-21.)

Note: Keep in mind that the type of writing done by the students determines the level of evaluation called for. Exploratory writing should be awarded a basic performance score plus a positive comment or two. A more complete writing project naturally demands more thorough assessment.

OBSERVATION/INTERACTION FORM FOR EXTENDED UNITS

(Note at least one significant observation or interaction for each student during the different stages of their work.)*

Student Names	PERCEIVING (Activities that introduce the unit)	IDEATING (Prewriting, writing, revising)	PRESENTING (Sharing finished products)

*Make note of your students' openness, eagerness, diligence, thoughtfulness, creativity, cooperativeness, and so on.

Evaluating Writing

Two kinds of evaluation interest teachers today: **formative evaluation** (evaluating while the students are developing their writing) and **summative evaluation** (evaluating the outcome of the students' efforts). Formative evaluation does not result in a grade; summative evaluation does. Some teachers choose, however, to give students a set number of points (a performance score) during different stages in the formative steps in the writing process.

FORMATIVE EVALUATION

Formative evaluation is most often used for writing-to-learn activities, prewriting activities, writing in progress, journal entries, and so forth. Three types of formative evaluation at the elementary level are widely used: the individual conference, the small-group conference, and peer conferencing.

THE INDIVIDUAL CONFERENCE

The individual conference can occur informally at the student's deskside, or it can take place at a scheduled time. In the early stages of the writing process, responses and questions should be about writing ideas, content, audience, purpose, generating ideas, and so on. Questions should be open-ended. This gives the writer "space" to talk. When a writer is talking, she is thinking, clarifying, and making decisions. Teachers don't have to attempt to solve problems for their students, but they can ask questions and suggest possible solutions.

In the editing and proofreading stage, a teacher might ask, "Why do you need a period here?" Students should try to answer the question and add the necessary punctuation marks. With the inexperienced writer, it's best not to mark all errors. Simply draw a double line to indicate where you stopped editing or proofreading the student's work. An individual conference can also be "student-directed" if a student finishes a draft, identifies a problem, or wants to share a breakthrough.

"Teachers need to look at each individual writer, and what's more, each writer will demonstrate different writing behaviors with different writing tasks."

—JoAnn Parry and David Hornsby
Write On: A Conference Approach to Writing

THE SMALL-GROUP CONFERENCE

The small-group conference may consist of groups of three to five students who are at the same stage of the writing process or who are involved in the same types of writing project. The goals of a small-group conference are to help students improve their own writing and to help students develop as evaluators of the writing of others. Minilessons work well in small-group conferences.

Consider holding a publisher's meeting during small-group conferences so students can help one another select writing to be published. Your role is to help students reach informed conclusions about their writing. For more about this type of evaluation, see ***Publishing Your Writing*** (pages 54-57), in *Writers Express*.

PEER CONFERENCING

Students need to learn how to conference with others (without the help of a teacher). We suggest that students at first work in pairs and use some type of evaluating checklist when they conference. Always model how to use an evaluating checklist before you have students use it. Impose a time limit for peer-responding sessions to keep students on task (10-15 minutes).

To help your students prepare for peer-conferencing sessions, have them read ***Conferencing with Partners*** (pages 42-45) and ***Sharing Family Stories*** (pages 46-49) in *Writers Express*.

One very simple process to use for peer responding is to ask a student to read his or her partner's paper and then generate three questions beginning with *who, what, where, when, why,* or *how*. The questions and paper are returned to the writer, who then responds to these questions. These questions serve as a starting point for a discussion. Students could also use one of the response sheets provided elsewhere in this section (pages 153-158).

> *"I used to think of writing as my most dreaded fear. Now it's what I look forward to. . . . When I look over my work, I feel honored that I wrote it."*
>
> —Kristen Tomlinson, grade 5

SUMMATIVE EVALUATION

We want students to value the writing process as much as if not more than the final product, and we want their attention to be on personal goals, not grades. However, the day will come when a grade must be assigned to at least some of their completed work. This is when summative evaluation is important. Here are some general principles to help you evaluate finished pieces.

1. Clearly establish the criteria for evaluating each piece of writing. Limit the criteria so you do not overwhelm the students or yourself.
2. Ask students to help you develop the criteria. This can be done in individual conferences or with the entire class. Students readily accept and understand criteria they have helped build.
3. Students must have ample opportunities for formative evaluation before their final products receive grades. And students deserve points for the work they have done during the writing process.
4. Concern for content, fluency, and fresh ideas should be given high priority during summative evaluation. Correctness is important, but it is only one part of the complete writing picture.
5. Students should be involved in summative evaluation. You can do this by providing students with a form that asks them to identify the best parts of their writing, list the problems they encountered, draw a circle around the parts they would work on if they had more time, and so on. In addition to the above ideas, students should be asked how much time they put into a project and what grade they would assign to it.

Suggested Reading for Evaluating Writing

Inside Out, Dan Kirby, Tom Liner

Learning to Write / Writing to Learn, John S. Mayher, Nancy Lester, Gordon M. Pradl

What Every Writer Needs, Ralph Fletcher

Write On: A Conference Approach to Writing, JoAnn Parry and David Hornsby

Approaches for Summative Evaluating

Analytic scales establish the features necessary for a successful piece of writing and attribute point values for each feature. The grade derives from the point total. Many students like this form of evaluation because it is concrete and it highlights specific strengths and weaknesses in their writing. The emphasis of analytic scales tends, however, to be on the parts rather than the whole.

Holistic grading evaluates a piece of writing as a whole. The most basic approach to holistic grading is to read the paper rather quickly for a general impression. The paper is graded according to this impression. A reader might also compare a particular piece with a number of pieces already graded, or grade it for the appearance of elements important to that type of writing. Holistic grading helps teachers reward creativity, inventiveness, and overall effect.

Task-specific scoring accords a grade based on how well a student has accomplished specific rhetorical tasks. A teacher might, for example, create a scoring checklist or guide for a short fiction writing assignment. This checklist would include those elements that are inherent in this writing form—plot, characterization, point of view, and so on. Students must understand the criteria for scoring before they begin their writing. This type of grading addresses specific rather than open-ended writing assignments.

Portfolio grading gives students an opportunity to choose pieces of writing to be graded. This is a common method of evaluation in writing workshops. Workshop students compile all their work in a portfolio or folder. Teachers require them to submit a specified number of finished projects for grading each quarter or semester. Students enjoy this method of evaluation because it gives them some control over the evaluation process; teachers like it because it lessens their workload since they don't have to grade everything a student has written.

A **performance system** is a quick and simple method of evaluation. If students complete a writing activity and it meets the previously established level of acceptability, they receive the preestablished grade or points for completing the assignment. The student either has completed the activity or he hasn't.

Using Writing Portfolios

More and more, language arts teachers are making portfolios an important part of their writing programs. Will portfolios work for you? Will they help you and your students assess their writing? Read on and find out.

What is a writing portfolio?

A writing portfolio is a limited collection of a student's writing for evaluation. A portfolio is different from the traditional writing folder (also known as a working folder), which contains all of a student's work. A portfolio contains only a student's best efforts.

Why should I ask students to compile writing portfolios?

Portfolios get students directly involved in the assessment process since they have to evaluate their own writing. Portfolios also make students accountable for their own writing progress. And they help students appreciate writing as an involved and recursive process of writing and rewriting.

You can employ any or all methods of assessment when portfolios are used, including self-evaluation, peer evaluation, contract writing, traditional grading, and so on.

How many pieces of writing should be included in a portfolio?

You and your students should really make that decision. You should, however, expect your students to compile at least three pieces of writing in a portfolio each quarter. (Some teachers have their students contract for a specific amount of required writing.) All drafts for each piece should be included. Generally, students are also required to include a reflective writing or self-critique sheet that assesses their writing progress.

Note: Some teachers want students to include in their portfolios one or two pieces of writing from other disciplines.

When do portfolios work best?

Students need plenty of class time to work on writing if they are going to produce effective portfolios. If they are used correctly, portfolios turn beginning writers into practicing writers. And practicing writers need regularly scheduled blocks of time to "practice" their craft.

Portfolios are tailor made for language arts classrooms that operate as writing workshops.

How can I help my students with their portfolio writing?

Give your students many opportunities to discuss their writing with their classmates. Make sharing sessions an important part of your class. Expect your students to evaluate their own writing and the writing of their peers—and help them to do so. (See ***Planning Your Portfolio*** in *Writers Express*.) Also provide students with guidance when they need help with their own writing. (Again, the handbook provides plenty of writing guidelines.) And create a stimulating classroom environment that encourages students to immerse themselves in writing.

How do I grade a portfolio?

Base each grade on goals you and your students establish at the beginning of the grading period and on what is achieved as evidenced in the portfolio. Many teachers develop a critique sheet for assessment that is based on the goals established by the class. (It's very important that students know how many pieces they should include in their portfolios, how their work should be arranged in their portfolios, how the portfolios will be assessed, and so on.)

Note: See pages 18-21 in the *Writers Express* handbook for student-directed material related to planning a portfolio.

Name ______________________ **RESPONSE SHEET**

Rating a Paper

DIRECTIONS: Use this response sheet when rating a writing partner's work.

Author's Name ______________________

Title ______________________

Rater's Name ______________________ Date ____________

The best part about this writing is ______________________

____

Three things that make this writing good

1. ______________________
2. ______________________
3. ______________________

Rating: 4 ________ 3 ________ 2 ________ 1 ________

This writing needs revision: Yes ______ No ______ If Yes, complete this form.

The part that I don't understand is ______________________

____

This writing could be improved by ______________________

____

RATING SCALE

4 – Excellent The writing has a beginning, a middle, and an end. All of the ideas are arranged in the best order, and there are enough details to support the subject. The writing contains interesting, descriptive words and ideas. The writing is free of careless errors.

3 – Good The writing has a beginning, a middle, and an end. Most of the ideas follow in order. A few details need to be added. The writing contains a few careless errors.

2 – Fair The writing doesn't have a clear beginning, middle, or end. It needs reorganizing. Main ideas aren't well developed. The writing contains careless errors.

1 – Weak The writing is not focused and contains many errors.

Name

RESPONSE SHEET

Memorable and More

DIRECTIONS: **Use this response sheet when working with a writing partner. Under "memorable" list things you really like about the writing. Under "more" list several suggestions or questions. (See page 45 in your handbook.)**

Memorable ______________________________

____

____

More ______________________________

____

____

Name

RESPONSE SHEET

Memorable and More

DIRECTIONS: **Use this response sheet when working with a writing partner. Under "memorable" list things you really like about the writing. Under "more" list several suggestions or questions. (See page 45 in your handbook.)**

Memorable ______________________________

____

____

More ______________________________

____

____

Name _______________ RESPONSE SHEET

Revising Checklist 1

DIRECTIONS: Use the following checklist as a guide when you review and revise a first draft.

1. ***Did I focus on a certain part of my subject, instead of trying to say everything about it?***

2. ***Do I need to add any information?***

    _____ Do I need to add a topic sentence or a sentence that states the main idea of my writing?

    _____ Do I need to add any important details?

    _____ Do I need to add a closing or concluding sentence?

3. ***Do I need to cut any information?***

    _____ Did I include any details that don't support my main idea?

    _____ Have I repeated myself in any parts?

    _____ Have I said too much about a certain idea?

4. ***Do I need to rewrite any parts?***

    _____ Are there ideas or sentences that are unclear or confusing?

    _____ Did I do too much telling and not enough showing?

    _____ Could I improve my explanation in a certain part?

5. ***Do I need to reorder any parts of my writing?***

    _____ Do any ideas or details seem to be out of place?

    _____ Did I place my most important point in the best spot?

    _____ Did I follow an effective method of organization?

Name ______________________ **RESPONSE SHEET**

Revising Checklist 2

DIRECTIONS: Use the following checklist as a guide when you review and revise second, third, and final drafts.

Organization:

_____ Does the writing have a beginning, a middle, and an end?

_____ Are all of the ideas arranged in the best order?

Details:

_____ Do all of the details support the subject (topic sentences)?

_____ Are enough details and examples included?

Style:

_____ Is the writing easy to follow?

_____ Does the writing contain interesting or descriptive words and ideas?

Mechanics:

_____ Is the writing accurate (free of careless spelling and punctuation errors)?

_____ Is the writing neatly presented?

Name

Editing and Proofreading Checklist

DIRECTIONS: Use this checklist as a guide when you edit your writing. Also use it when you are ready to proofread your final draft.

Sentence Structure

______ Did I write clear and complete sentences?

______ Did I write sentences of different lengths?

______ Did I begin my sentences in different ways?

Punctuation

______ Does each sentence end with an end punctuation mark?

______ Did I use commas in a series (*Larry, Moe, and Curly*)?

______ Did I place commas before connecting words (*and, but, or, so*) in compound sentences?

______ Did I punctuate dialogue correctly? (See pages 346 and 350 in *Writers Express* for help.)

Capitalization

______ Did I start all my sentences with a capital letter?

______ Did I capitalize nouns that name specific people, places, and things?

Usage

______ Did I use powerful verbs, specific nouns, and colorful modifiers?

______ Did I use the correct word (*to, too,* or *two; your* or *you're*)? (See pages 362-369 in your handbook for help.)

Spelling

______ Did I check for spelling? Did I use the spell-checker on my computer? (See pages 270-273 in your handbook for help.)

SPELLING RULES

Name ______________________ **RESPONSE SHEET**

Writing a Report: A Summary Checklist

DIRECTIONS: Use this checklist as a guide whenever you write a report.

Select a Good Topic

_____ 1. Create a web (list, cluster).

_____ 2. Let your web sit.

_____ 3. Ask general questions.

_____ 4. Ask specific questions.

Collect Information

_____ 1. Use a gathering grid.

_____ 2. Ask open-ended questions.

_____ 3. Find good sources of information.

_____ 4. Answer your questions.

_____ 5. Use note cards, if needed.

_____ 6. Check your information.

Connect Your Ideas

_____ 1. Begin with a hook.

_____ 2. Tie your facts together.

_____ 3. Use quotes and charts.

_____ 4. End with a strong point.

_____ 5. List your sources.

Check Your Report

_____ 1. Have you used clear, complete sentences?

_____ 2. Are your paragraphs well organized?

_____ 3. Have you covered the topic completely?

_____ 4. Have you used quotation marks correctly?

_____ 5. Have you checked your spelling, usage, and punctuation?

_____ 6. Is your report written (or typed) neatly?

Reading-Writing Connection

In "Reading-Writing Connection," you will find lists of important, high-interest titles that relate to many chapters in *Writers Express.* These lists will prove invaluable when planning extended units for these chapters. Also included in this section are two masters that will help students keep track of their reading progress.

Sharing Family Stories

All-of-a-Kind Family
Sydney Taylor, 1951

Appalachia: The Voices of Sleeping Birds Ⓔ
Cynthia Rylant, 1991

Astrid Lindgren: Storyteller to the World Ⓔ
Johanna Hurwitz, 1989

Families: A Celebration of Diversity, Commitment, and Love
Aylette Jenness, 1990

Go and Catch a Flying Fish Ⓔ
Mary Stolz, 1991

The Hundred-Penny Box Ⓔ
Sharon Bell Mathis, 1975

I'm in Charge of Celebrations Ⓔ
Byrd Baylor, 1986

Journey
Patricia MacLachlan, 1991

The Moon Lady Ⓔ
Amy Tan, 1992

Owl Moon Ⓔ
Jane Yolen, 1987

Pueblo Storyteller
Diane Hoyt-Goldsmith, 1991

The Remembering Box
Eth Clifford, 1985

Song and Dance Man Ⓔ
Karen Ackerman, 1988

Song of the Trees
Mildred Taylor, 1975

Three Names Ⓔ
Patricia MacLachlan, 1991

Ⓒ = Challenging Ⓔ = Easy

Writing in Journals

Anastasia Krupnik Ⓒ
Lois Lowry, 1979

Arthur, for the Very First Time
Patricia MacLachlan, 1980

Cassie Binegar
Patricia MacLachlan, 1982

Celia's Island Journal Ⓔ
Celia Thaxter (adapted by Loretta Krupinski), 1992

Chasing After Annie
Marjorie Weinman Sharmat, 1981

Dear Mr. Henshaw
Beverly Cleary, 1983

Harriet the Spy
Louise Fitzhugh, 1964

Hey World, Here I Am!
Jean Little, 1989

I'm in Charge of Celebrations Ⓔ
Byrd Baylor, 1986

Linnea's Almanac Ⓔ
Christina Bjork, 1989

Mr. and Mrs. Thief Ⓔ
Naomi Kojima, 1980

Mostly Michael
Robert Kimmel Smith, 1987

Sister
Eloise Greenfield, 1974

Zlata's Diary: A Child's Life in Sarajevo
Zlata Filipovic, 1994

Writing Book Reviews

Arthur, for the Very First Time
Patricia MacLachlan, 1980

Bridge to Terabithia
Katherine Paterson, 1977

The True Confessions of Charlotte Doyle Ⓒ
Avi, 1990

Ⓒ = Challenging Ⓔ = Easy

Writing Personal Narratives

The Best Town in the World
Byrd Baylor, 1986

Bigmama's Ⓔ
Donald Crews, 1991

Bill Peet: An Autobiography
Bill Peet, 1989

Childtimes: A Three-Generation Memoir
Eloise Greenfield and Lessie Jones Little, 1993

Don't You Know There's a War On? Ⓔ
James Stevenson, 1992

A Forever Family
Roslyn Banish, with Jennifer Jordan-Wong, 1992

A Grain of Wheat
Clyde Robert Bulla, 1985

Journey to Jo'burg: A South African Story
Beverley Naidoo, 1986

Homesick: My Own Story
Jean Fritz, 1982

I'm the Big Sister Now
Michelle Emmert, 1989

Little By Little: A Writer's Education Ⓒ
Jean Little, 1987

The Moon and I
Betsy Byars, 1992

Nana Upstairs and Nana Downstairs Ⓔ
Tomie dePaola, 1978

The Relatives Came Ⓔ
Cynthia Rylant, 1993

Stars Come Out Within Ⓒ
Jean Little, 1990

War Boy: A Country Childhood Ⓔ
Michael Foreman, 1990

When I Was Young in the Mountains Ⓔ
Cynthia Rylant, 1985

Writing Letters

Dear Annie
Judith Caseley, 1991

Dear Brother Ⓔ
Frank Asch, 1992

Dear Dad, Love Laurie
Susan Beth Pfeffer, 1989

Dear Dr. Bell. . . Your Friend, Helen Keller
Judith St. George, 1992

Dear Emily
Maureen Stewart, 1986

Dearest Grandmama Ⓔ
Catherine Brighton, 1991

Dear Mr. Henshaw
Beverly Cleary, 1983

Dear Napoleon, I Know You're Dead But. . .
Elvira Woodruff, 1992

The Jolly Postman Ⓔ
Janet and Allan Ahlberg, 1986

A Letter to Amy Ⓔ
Ezra Jack Keats, 1968

Letters of Thanks
Manghanita Kempadoo, 1969

Mailbox Quailbox Ⓔ
Margaret Ronay Legum, 1985

Modest Proposals: The Official Correspondence of Randy Cohen Ⓒ
Randy Cohen, 1981

Penny Pollard's Letters Ⓒ
Robin Klein, 1984

Sarah, Plain and Tall
Patricia MacLachlan, 1985

Your Best Friend, Kate Ⓔ
Pat Brisson, 1989

Writing Explanations

Farmer Boy
Laura Ingalls Wilder, 1971

Freckle Juice
Judy Blume, 1978

Hatchet Ⓒ
Gary Paulsen, 1988

Johnny Tremain
Esther Forbes, 1987

Little House in the Big Woods
Laura Ingalls Wilder, 1971

Soda Poppery Ⓒ
Stephen Tchudi, 1986

Trouble River
Betsy Byars, 1989

Ⓒ = Challenging Ⓔ = Easy

Writing Fantasies

Attic Mice Ⓔ
Ethel Pochocki, 1993

Babe, the Gallant Pig
Dick King-Smith, 1983

Catwings Ⓔ
Ursula K. LeGuin, 1988

Charlie and the Chocolate Factory Ⓒ
Roald Dahl, 1964

The Computer Nut
Betsy Byars, 1984

The Dragon's Boy
Jane Yolen, 1990

Flat Stanley Ⓔ
Jeff Brown, 1964

The Garden of Abdul Gasazi Ⓔ
Chris Van Allsburg, 1979

Haunting Ⓒ
Margaret Mahy, 1982

The Hoboken Chicken Emergency
Daniel M. Pinkwater, 1977

Inside My Feet: The Story of a Giant
Richard Kennedy, 1991

The King's Equal Ⓔ
Katherine Paterson, 1992

Knights of the Kitchen Table
Jon Scieszka, 1993

The Lion, the Witch, and the Wardrobe Ⓒ
C. S. Lewis, 1950

Lucie Babbidge's House Ⓒ
Sylvia Cassedy, 1989

Mrs. Frisby and the Rats of NIMH
Robert C. O'Brien, 1971

Nonstop Nonsense
Margaret Mahy, 1977

The Magic School Bus Inside the Human Body Ⓔ
Joanna Cole, 1988

The Old Banjo Ⓔ
Dennis Haseley, 1983

Redwall Ⓒ
Brian Jacques, 1986

Roxaboxen Ⓔ
Alice McLerran, 1991

A String in the Harp Ⓒ
Nancy Bond, 1976

A Wrinkle in Time Ⓒ
Madeleine L'Engle, 1962

Writing Tall Tales

American Indian Myths and Legends Ⓒ
Edited by Richard Erdoes and Alfonso Ortiz, 1984

Cut From the Same Cloth: American Women of Myth, Legend, and Tall Tale
Robert D. San Souci, 1993

The Elephant's Bathtub: Wonder Tales from the Far East
Frances Carpenter, 1962

Febold Feboldson Ⓔ
Arian Dewey, 1984

Fin M'Coul: The Giant of Knockmany Hill Ⓔ
Tomie dePaola, 1981

How Glooskap Outwits the Ice Giant and the Other Tales of the Maritime Indians Ⓒ
Howard Norman, 1989

Iva Dunnit and the Big Wind Ⓔ
by Carol Purdy, 1985

John Henry: Steel-driving Man
C. J. Naden, 1980

Johnny Appleseed Ⓔ
Steven Kellogg, 1992

The Kingdom Under the Sea and Other Stories Ⓒ
Joan Aiken, 1986

Mr. Yowder and the Train Robbers
Glen Rounds, 1981

Paul Bunyan
Louis Sabin, 1985

Pecos Bill Ⓔ
Steven Kellogg, 1986

Sally Ann Thunder Ann Whirlwind Crockett
Caron Lee Cohen, 1993

Ⓒ = Challenging Ⓔ = Easy

Writing Realistic Stories

Afternoon of the Elves
Janet Taylor Lisle, 1989

All the Money in the World
Bill Brittain, 1979

Are You There God, It's Me, Margaret Ⓒ
Judy Blume, 1970

A Blue-Eyed Daisy
Cynthia Rylant, 1985

The Cat Ate My Gymsuit Ⓒ
Paula Danzinger, 1980

The Cay Ⓒ
Theodore Taylor, 1987

The Christmas Cup Ⓔ
Nancy Ruth Patterson, 1989

Felita
Nicholasa Mohr, 1979

Fourth Grade Rats Ⓔ
Jerry Spinelli, 1991

The Gift Ⓒ
Joan Lowery Nixon, 1983

Goodbye, Vietnam
by Gloria Whelan, 1993

Goodbye My Island
Jean Rogers, 1983

Hot and Cold Summer
Johanna Hurwitz, 1984

The Hundred Dresses
Eleanor Estes, 1944

It's Like This, Cat Ⓒ
Emily Cheney Neville, 1991

Journey
Patricia MacLachlan, 1991

Kid Power
Susan Pfeffer, 1977

King Shoes and Clown Pockets Ⓒ
Faye Gibbons, 1989

The Not-Just-Anybody Family
(and sequels)
Betsy Byars, 1986

Me, Mop, and the Moondance Kid
Walter Dean Myers, 1988

Miracle at the Plate
Matt Christopher, 1967

Mississippi Bridge
Mildred D. Taylor, 1990

Mrs. Fish, Ape, and Me, The Dump Queen
Norma Fox Mazer, 1980

My Side of the Mountain Ⓒ
Jean George, 1988

Ramona Forever Ⓔ
Beverly Cleary, 1979

Roll of Thunder, Hear My Cry Ⓒ
Mildred D. Taylor, 1976

Shoeshine Girl Ⓔ
Clyde Robert Bulla, 1975

Soup
Robert Newton Peck, 1974

Stone Fox Ⓔ
John R. Gardiner, 1980

A Summer to Die
Lois Lowry, 1977

A Taste of Blackberries
Doris B. Smith, 1973

Thirteen Ways to Sink a Sub Ⓔ
Jamie Gilson, 1982

The Wall
Eve Bunting, 1990

Writing Stories from History

And Then What Happened, Paul Revere?
Jean Fritz, 1973
[American Revolution]

The Cabin Faced West
Jean Fritz, 1958
[American frontier]

The Courage of Sarah Noble Ⓔ
Alice Dalgliesh, 1954
[18th-century America]

Dawn of Fear Ⓒ
Susan Cooper, 1970
[Horror of war/England]

Double Life of Pocahontas
Jean Fritz, 1983
[Colonial America]

A Gift for Mama
Esther Hautzig, 1981
[Jewish perspective pre-WWII]

I Am Regina Ⓒ
Sally M. Keehn, 1991
[French/Indian War]

The Iron Dragon Never Sleeps Ⓔ
Stephen Krensky, 1994
[Post-Civil War West]

Jar of Dreams
Yoshiko Uchida, 1981
[Depression/America]

Jim Ugly
Sid Fleischman, 1992
[Old West/America]

Katie's Trunk Ⓔ
Ann Turner, 1992
[American Revolution]

Lion to Guard Us
Clyde Robert Bulla, 1981
[Colonial America]

Little House on the Prairie
Laura Ingalls Wilder, 1953
[American frontier]

My Name is Not Angelica Ⓒ
Scott O'Dell, 1990
[18th-century slavery]

Morning Girl Ⓒ
Michael Dorris, 1992
[15th-century America]

Number the Stars
Lois Lowry, 1989
[World War II]

Pocahontas and the Strangers
Clyde Robert Bulla, 1971
[Colonial America]

The Printer's Apprentice Ⓔ
Stephen Krensky, 1995
[Colonial America]

Sadako and the Thousand Paper Cranes
Eleanor Coerr, 1977
[Nuclear war]

Sarah, Plain and Tall
Patricia MacLachlan, 1985
[American frontier]

The Secret Soldier: The Story of Deborah Sampson Ⓔ
Ann McGovern, 1975
[American Revolution]

Trouble River
Betsy Byars, 1969
[American frontier]

When Hitler Stole Pink Rabbit
Judith Kerr, 1971
[World War II]

Ⓒ = Challenging Ⓔ = Easy

Writing Poems

And the Green Grass Grew All Around: Folk Poetry for Everyone Ⓔ
Collected by Alvin Schwartz, 1992

The Book of Pigericks Ⓔ
Arnold Lobel, 1983

Celebration: The Story of American Holidays Ⓔ
Lucille Recht Penner, 1993

Click, Rumble, Roar: Poems About Machines
Selected by Lee Bennett Hopkins, 1987

Creatures of Earth, Sea, and Sky
Georgia Heard, 1992

Dinosaur Dances
Jane Yolen, 1990

Dogs and Dragons, Trees and Dreams
Karla Kuskin, 1980

Hey World, Here I Am!
Jean Little, 1989

Eats Poems
Arnold Adoff, 1979

Honey, I Love and Other Love Poems
Eloise Greenfield, 1978

If You're Not Here, Please Raise Your Hand
Kalli Dakos, 1990

Joyful Noise: Poems for Two Voices
Paul Fleischman, 1988

My Song is Beautiful: Poems and Pictures in Many Voices Ⓔ
Selected by Mary Ann Hoberman, 1994

The Random House Book of Poetry for Children
Jack Prelutsky, 1983

Rainbow Writing
Eve Merriam, 1976

Song in Stone: City Poems
Edited by Lee Bennett Hopkins

Somebody Catch My Homework
David Harrison, 1993

Street Rhymes Around the World
Jane Yolen, 1992

The Trees Stand Shining: Poetry of the North American Indians
Collected by Hettie Jones, 1993

Through Our Eyes: Poems and Pictures About Growing Up
Selected by Lee Bennett Hopkins, 1992

Where Fish Go in Winter and Answers to Other Mysteries
Amy Goldman Koss, 1987

Wind in the Long Grass: A Collection of Haiku Ⓒ
Edited by William J. Higginson, 1992

Writing Songs

The American Songbag Ⓒ
Carl Sandberg, 1990

Folksongs of North America Ⓒ
Alan Lomax, 1975

Gonna Sing My Head Off! Ⓔ
Collected and arranged by Kathleen Krull, 1992

I'm Going to Sing: Black American Spirituals
Collected by Bryan Ashley, 1982

On the Riverbank Ⓔ
Charles Temple, 1992

Writing Plays

Aesop's Fables: Plays for Young Children
Dr. Albert Cullum, 1993

Greek and Roman Plays for the Intermediate Grades Ⓒ
Dr. Albert Cullum, 1994

Plays: The Drama Magazine for Young People
Published by Plays, Inc.

Ⓒ = Challenging Ⓔ = Easy

Writing Riddles

Eight Ate: A Feast of Homonym Riddles
Marvin Terban, 1982

Funny You Should Ask: How to Make Up Jokes and Riddles with Wordplay
Marvin Terban, 1992

Geographunny
Mort Gerberg, 1991

Hey, Hay! A Wagonful of Funny Homonym Riddles
Marvin Terban, 1990

How Do You Get a Horse Out of a Bathtub?
Louis Phillips, 1983

Ji-Nongo-Nongo Means Riddles Ⓔ
Verna Aardema, 1978

Petcetera: The Pet Riddle Book Ⓔ
Meyer Seltzer, 1988

Riddle Roundup Ⓔ
Giulio Maestro, 1989

Ridiculous Nicholas Pet Riddles Ⓔ
Joseph Rosenbloom, 1981

Riddles to Tell Your Cat Ⓔ
Caroline Levine, 1992

Unriddling: All Sorts of Riddles to Puzzle Your Guessery
Edited by Alvin Schwartz, 1983

Westward Ho Ho Ho! Jokes from the Wild West
Victoria Hartman, 1993

What's a Frank Frank? Tasty Homograph Riddles
Giulio Maestro, 1984

Writing for Fun

Autographs! I Collect Them Ⓔ
Michael Frith, 1974

Cross Your Fingers, Spit in Your Hat: Superstitions and Other Beliefs
Alvin Schwartz, 1974

Go Hang a Salami! I'm a Lasagna Hog! and Other Palindromes
Jon Agee, 1993

Kids' Random Acts of Kindness Ⓒ
Editors of Conari Press, 1994

The Ramona Quimby Diary
Beverly Cleary, 1984

The Travel Bug: A Travel Journey for Kids 7-14
Linda Schwartz, 1993

Writing a Classroom Report

The Amazing Potato: A Story in Which the Incas, Conquistadors, Marie Antoinette, Thomas Jefferson, Wars, Famines, Immigrants, and French Fries All Play a Part Ⓒ
Milton Melzer, 1992

How on Earth Do We Recycle Paper?
Helen Jill Fletcher and Seli Groves, 1993

It Happened in America: True Stories from the Fifty States Ⓒ
Lila Perl, 1993

The Last Princess: The Story of Princess Ka'iulani of Hawaii Ⓔ
Fay Stanley, 1992

Lights! Camera! Action! How a Movie is Made
Gail Gibbons, 1985

A River Ran Wild: An Environmental History Ⓔ
Lynne Cherry, 1993

Season of the Cranes
Peter Roop, 1989

Surrounded by Sea: Life On a New England Fishing Island Ⓔ
Gail Gibbons, 1991

Talking Walls Ⓔ
Margy Burns Knight, 1992

We the People: The Constitution of the United States of America Ⓔ
Peter Spier, 1987

Weather Forecasting Ⓒ
Gail Gibbons, 1993

Weather Words and What They Mean Ⓔ
Gail Gibbons, 1990

Where on Earth: A Geografunny Guide to the Globe
Paul Rosenthal, 1993

The Historical Time Line

Time Lines: Entertainment
Jacqueline Morley, 1994

Time Lines: Flight
David Jefferis, 1994

Time Lines: Inventions
Peter Turvey, 1994

Time Lines: Food
Richard Tames, 1994

Ⓒ = Challenging Ⓔ = Easy

Reading-Homework Contract

I am expected to read at home for at least ____________________ .

I know that this is a yearlong assignment and that I may sometimes have additional reading assignments.

I understand that I may choose the books and also the times and the days that I will read. I also understand that during this reading-homework time, I am to read well-selected material. (Certain magazines, comic books, catalogs, and picture books are not acceptable.)

☐ I did read and understand the above information. I can keep track of my own reading homework and will report it on the reverse side of this sheet.

☐ I did read and understand the above information. I will have someone at home help me keep track of and report my reading homework.

____
(Student signature)

____
(date)

____
(Teacher signature)

____
(date)

I have discussed this contract with my child and agree that his/her choice (above) is appropriate.

____
(Parent signature)

____
(date)

Note to parents: If you have any questions about this homework contract, please feel free to call me.

BOOKS I HAVE READ

BOOK TITLE	Number of Pages	Author	I give this book ★ / ★★ / ★★★ / ★★★★

Bibliography

In the bibliography you will find references and resource titles for each chapter in the handbook. Turn here for help whenever you are interested in gathering more information related to a particular chapter.

THE PROCESS OF WRITING

Getting Started

REFERENCES

All About Writing

Graves, Donald. *Writing: Teachers and Children at Work.* Portsmouth: Heinemann, 1983.

One Writer's Process & A Basic Writing Guide

Murray, Donald M. *Learning by Teaching.* Upper Montclair: Boynton Cook, 1982.

Writing with a Computer

Ferguson, Marilyn. "Introduction to Chapter One." *Writing and Technology: Ideas That Work!* Ed. Sharon Franklin. Eugene: Visions for Learning, 1993.

Planning Your Portfolio

Rief, Linda. "Finding the Value in Portfolios." *Seeking Diversity: Language Arts with Adolescents.* Portsmouth: Heinemann, 1992.

RESOURCES

Anthony, Robert, et al. *Evaluating Literacy: A Perspective for Change.* Portsmouth: Heinemann, 1991. (Guidelines and processes for gathering information are practical. Issues that won't go away, such as letter grades, are discussed.)

Calkins, Lucy M. *The Art of Teaching Writing.* 2nd ed. Portsmouth: Heinemann, 1994. (Provides an updated and completely rewritten second edition of this title, with added chapters on assessment, reading-writing relationships, and more)

Golub, Jeffrey N. "Computers in English Instruction." *Activities for an Interactive Classroom.* Urbana: National Council of Teachers of English, 1994. (Provides a chapter on using the word processor for revision)

Potter, Shelly. *Portfolios and Student-Led Conferencing.* Birmingham: Potter Press, 1992. (Specific strategies and helpful blackline masters for parent-teacher-student conferences)

Prewriting and Drafting Guide

REFERENCES

Building a File of Writing Ideas

Dakos, Kalli. *What's There to Write About?* New York: Scholastic, 1989.

Selecting a Subject

Tchudi, Susan, and Stephen Tchudi. *The Young Writer's Handbook*. New York: Charles Scribner's Sons, 1984.

Starting Points for Writing

Kovacs, Deborah, and James Preller. *Meet the Authors and Illustrators: 60 Creators of Favorite Children's Books Talk About Their Work*. New York: Scholastic, 1991.

Collecting Details

Elbow, Peter. *Writing with Power: Techniques for Mastering the Writing Process*. New York: Oxford University Press, 1981.

Planning and Drafting Tips

Murray, Donald M. *Write to Learn*. New York: Holt, Rinehart & Winston, 1984.

Building a Resource of Writing Forms

Moffett, James, and Betty J. Wagner. *Student-Centered Language Arts and Reading, K-12*. Boston: Houghton Mifflin, 1976.

RESOURCES

Asher, Sandy. *Where Do You Get Your Ideas?* New York: Walker and Company, 1993. (Techniques for generating writing ideas are discussed by Asher and other writers [Lois Lowery, Patricia Reilly Giff, etc.].)

Fletcher, Ralph. *What a Writer Needs*. Portsmouth: Heinemann, 1993. (Offers short essays on the writer's craft, from the art of using details to developing voice and significant subjects)

Rico, Gabriele L. *Writing the Natural Way: Using Right-Brain Techniques to Release Your Expressive Powers.* Los Angeles: Tarcher, 1983. (See, especially, chapter 2, "Clustering: Doorway to Your Design Mind.")

Revising and Editing Guide

REFERENCES

Revising Your Writing

Murray, Donald M. *Learning by Teaching.* Upper Montclair: Boynton Cook, 1982.

Conferencing with Partners

Nathan, Ruth, et al. *Classroom Strategies that Work: An Elementary Teacher's Guide to Process Writing.* Portsmouth: Heinemann, 1989.

Sharing Family Stories

Ponsot, Marie, and Rosemary Deen. *The Common Sense: What to Write, How to Write It, and Why.* Upper Montclair: Boynton Cook, 1985.

Editing and Proofreading

Sebranek, Patrick, Verne Meyer, and Dave Kemper. *Write Source 2000: A Guide to Writing, Thinking, & Learning.* Boston: D.C. Heath and Company, a Houghton Mifflin Company, 1995.

Publishing Your Writing

Henderson, Kathy. *The Market Guide for Young Writers.* 4th ed. Cincinnati: Writer's Digest Books, 1993.

RESOURCES

Asher, Sandy. *Wild Words! How to Train Them to Tell Stories.* New York: Walker and Company, 1989. (Many examples of what to do, and why, when revising)

Kirby, Dan, and Tom Liner. *Inside Out: Developmental Strategies for Teaching Writing.* Upper Montclair: Boynton Cook, 1981. (Offers the best strategies for revising)

Strunk, William, and E. B. White. *The Elements of Style.* 3rd ed. New York: Macmillan, 1979. (A classic reference filled with revising and editing suggestions)

Willis, Meredith S. *Deep Revision: A Guide for Teachers, Students, and Other Writers.* New York: Teachers & Writers Collaborative, 1993. (Many innovative techniques for helping students "re-view" their writing)

Building Paragraphs and Essays

REFERENCES

Writing Paragraphs

Donald, Robert B., et al. *Writing Clear Paragraphs*. Englewood Cliffs: Prentice-Hall, 1978.

Writing Essays

Graves, Donald H. *Investigate Nonfiction*. Portsmouth: Heinemann, 1989.

A Writing Sampler

Gould, June. *The Writer in All of Us*. New York: Dutton, 1989.

RESOURCES

Moffett, James. *Active Voices I*. Upper Montclair: Boynton Cook, 1987. (A broad-based collection of students' writing in many forms)

Ponsot, Marie, and Rosemary Deen. *The Common Sense*: *What to Write, How to Write it, and Why.* Upper Montclair: Boynton Cook, 1985. (Provides seed sentences based on personal knowledge that lead to several useful essay forms)

Sebranek, Patrick, Verne Meyer, and Dave Kemper. *Writers INC: A Guide to Writing, Thinking, & Learning.* Boston: D.C. Heath and Company, a Houghton Mifflin Company, 1996. (Specific advice for writing all types of sentences, paragraphs, and larger forms; a good teacher reference)

Improving Your Writing Skills

REFERENCES

Combining Sentences

Strong, William. *Sentence Combining and Paragraph Building*. New York: McGraw, 1981.

Writing with Style

Zinsser, William. *On Writing Well: An Informal Guide to Writing Nonfiction*. New York: Harper & Row, 1985.

Modeling the Masters

Asher, Sandy. *Where Do You Get Your Ideas?* New York: Walker and Company, 1993.

Copeland, Jeffrey S. *Speaking of Poets: Interviews with Poets Who Write for Children and Young Adults*. Urbana: National Council of Teachers of English, 1993.

Henderson, Kathy. *The Market Guide for Young Writers.* 4th ed. Cincinnati: Writer's Digest Books, 1993.

RESOURCES

Gray, James, and Robert Benson. *Sentence and Paragraph Modeling*. Berkeley: The Bay Area Writing Project, 1982. (Provides examples and insights into modeling professional writers)

Polette, Nancy. *The Best Ever Writing Models From Children's Literature*. St. Louis: Gateway Printing, 1989. (Provides excerpts from well-known children's literature, with guidelines on what to look for as students model the masters)

Stewig, John Warren. *Read to Write: Using Children's Literature As a Springboard for Teaching and Writing.* 3rd ed. Katonah: R. Owen, 1990. (This book provides lessons on all aspects of fiction and poetry.)

Personal Writing

REFERENCES

Writing in Journals

Atwell, Nancie, ed. *Coming to Know: Writing to Learn in the Intermediate Grades*. Portsmouth: Heinemann, 1990.

Writing Personal Narratives

Asher, Sandy. *Wild Words! How to Train Them to Tell Stories*. New York: Walker and Company, 1989.

Writing Friendly Letters

Applegate, Mauree. "Letters Are Self-Stamped." *Easy in English*. Evanston: Harper & Row, 1960.

James, Elizabeth, and Carol Barkin. *Sincerely Yours: How to Write Great Letters*. New York: Clarion Books, 1993.

RESOURCES

Fulwiler, Toby, ed. *The Journal Book*. Portsmouth: Heinemann, 1987. (A book describing how journals help students think, testing their own and others' ideas against experience)

Stevens, Carla. *A Book of Your Own: Keeping a Diary or Journal*. New York: Clarion Books, 1993. (This book tells students everything they need to know in order to start a diary or journal. Many examples from famous children are included.)

United States Postal Service and the National Council of Teachers of English. *P.S. Write Soon! All About Letters.* Urbana: U.S. Postal Service and National Council of Teachers of English, 1982. (A booklet devoted solely to all forms of letter writing, including sections on making stationery and communicating in braille)

Subject Writing

REFERENCES

Writing Newspaper Stories

Clark, Roy P. *Free to Write: A Journalist Teaches Young Writers*. Portsmouth: Heinemann, 1987.

Graves, Donald H. "The Lively Art of the Interview." *Investigate Nonfiction*. Portsmouth: Heinemann, 1989.

Writing Book Reviews

James, Elizabeth, and Carol Barkin. *How to Write Your Best Book Report*. New York: Lothrop, Lee & Shepard Books, 1986.

Writing Business Letters

United States Postal Service and the National Council of Teachers of English. *P.S. Write Soon! All About Letters*. Urbana: U.S. Postal Service and National Council of Teachers of English, 1982.

Writing Observation Reports

Caplan, Rebekah. *Writers in Training*. Palo Alto: Dale Seymour Publications, 1984.

RESOURCES

Granfield, Linda. *Extra! Extra! The Who, What, Where, When and Why of Newspapers*. New York: Orchard Books, 1992. (A book telling all the whos, whats, wheres, whens, and whys of newspaper writing)

Graves, Donald H. *Investigate Nonfiction*. Portsmouth: Heinemann, 1989. (See chapter 2, "Transitions from Oral Forms to Reading and Writing," for strategies to help children write observations.)

Liddelow, Lorelei. *Cook With Me*. Manitoba, Canada: Peguis, 1990. (Offers a wide variety of fun activities centered around cooking with children; useful for learning to write explanations)

Stone Soup: The Magazine by Children. Santa Cruz: Children's Art Foundation. (A magazine devoted to children's writing that often contains book reviews)

The Student Environmental Action Coalition. *Student Environmental Action Guide*. Berkeley: The Earth Works Group, 1991. (Activities include writing business letters)

Writing Tales and Stories

REFERENCES

Writing Fantasies

Tchudi, Susan, and Stephen Tchudi. *The Young Writer's Handbook*. New York: Charles Scribner's Sons, 1984.

Writing Tall Tales

Hamilton, Martha, and Mitch Weiss. "How to Make Story Telling an Integral Part of Your Curriculum." *Children Tell Stories: A Teaching Guide*. Katonah: R. Owen, 1990.

Writing Realistic Stories

Asher, Sandy. *Wild Words! How to Train Them to Tell Stories*. New York: Walker and Company, 1989.

Writing Stories from History

Tunnell, Michael O., and Richard Ammon. *The Story of Ourselves: Teaching History Through Children's Literature*. Portsmouth: Heinemann, 1993.

Weitzman, David. *My Backyard History Book*. Boston: Little, Brown, 1975.

RESOURCES

Lukens, Rebecca J. *A Critical Handbook of Children's Literature*. 4th ed. Glenview: Scott Foresman, 1990. (Provides a clear and direct explanation of all aspects of children's literature)

Moss, Joy F. "Bird Tales: Fact and Fiction." *Focus on Literature: A Context for Literacy Learning*. Katonah: R. Owen, 1990. (Shows teachers and children how to combine fact and fiction to produce realistic stories)

Moss, Joy F. *Using Literature in the Middle Grades: A Thematic Approach*. Norwood: Christopher-Gordon, 1991. (See chapters 4 and 7, "Dilemmas and Decisions: Internal Conflict in Realistic Fiction" and "War and Peace: Historical Fiction and Nonfiction," for detailed reading/writing strategies.)

Willis, Meredith Sue. *Personal Fiction Writing*. New York: Teachers & Writers Collaborative, 1984.

Zarnowski, Myra. "Helping Students Write Historical Fiction." *Activities to Promote Critical Thinking*. Ed. Jeff Golub, Chair of the Committee on Classroom Practices. Urbana: National Council of Teachers of English, 1986. (Offers a four-part procedure for writing historical fiction)

Writing Poems, Plays, and Songs

REFERENCES

Writing Poems

Copeland, Jeffrey S. *Speaking of Poets: Interviews with Poets Who Write for Children and Young Adults*. Urbana: National Council of Teachers of English, 1993.

Stafford, William. *Writing the Australian Crawl: Views on the Writer's Vocation*. Ann Arbor: University of Michigan Press, 1978.

Writing Plays

Asher, Sandy. "The Elements of Playwriting." *Writers in the Classroom*. Ed. Ruth Nathan. Norwood: Christopher-Gordon, 1991.

Writing for Fun

Stillman, Peter. *Families Writing*. Cincinnati: Writer's Digest Books, 1989.

RESOURCES

Geller, Linda Gibson. *Word Play and Language Learning for Children*. Urbana: National Council of Teachers of English, 1985. (See the playful writing activities for the middle years on pages 55-94.)

Gillette, Steve. *Songwriting and the Creative Process: Starting Points for Songwriters.* Bethlehem: Sing Out!, 1995. (Offers basic musical instruction followed by explanations of different genres and steps to the songwriting process)

Heard, Georgia. *For the Good of the Earth and Sun: Teaching Poetry*. Portsmouth: Heinemann, 1989. (This book's strength is in its sincerity, in its informed vision of how to inspire students to want to write poetry, and in the author's approaches to conferencing.)

Moffett, James, and Betty J. Wagner. *Student-Centered Language Arts, K-12*. Portsmouth: Heinemann, 1992. (See the activities incorporating songs and riddles.)

Sklar, Daniel J. *Playmaking: Children Writing & Performing Their Own Plays*. New York: Teachers & Writers Collaborative, 1991. (Twenty basic lessons offering a step-by-step account of how the author teaches children to write, direct, and perform their own plays—as staged readings, videotapes, radio plays, and full-stage productions)

Terban, Marvin. *Funny You Should Ask: How to Make Up Jokes and Riddles with Wordplay*. New York: Clarion Books, 1992.

Research Writing

REFERENCES

Writing a Classroom Report

James, Elizabeth, and Carol Barkin. *How to Write a Great School Report*. New York: Beech Tree Books, 1983.

Tchudi, Stephen. "Planning for Interdisciplinary Teaching." *Travels Across the Curriculum: Models for Interdisciplinary Learning*. New York: Scholastic, 1991.

RESOURCES

Brownlie, Faye, Susan Close, and Linda Wingren. *Tomorrow's Classroom Today: Strategies for Creating Active Readers, Writers, and Thinkers*. Portsmouth: Heinemann, 1990. (See chapter 7, "Listen—Sketch—Draft," for a helpful approach to this type of writing.)

Tchudi, Stephen, ed. *The Astonishing Curriculum: Integrating Science and Humanities Through Language*. Urbana: National Council of Teachers of English, 1993. (School projects come alive as these teachers bridge the gap between science and humanities. Students, often through writing, construct and explain their own knowledge, creating a language base for learning.)

Ward, Geoff, ed. *I've Got a Project On . . . .* Rozelle, Australia: PETA (Portsmouth: Heinemann, 1988). (Offers specific guidelines on every aspect of project development, from doing research to involving parents—very practical)

Wilde, Jack. *A Door Opens: Writing in Fifth Grade*. Portsmouth: Heinemann, 1993. (Using classroom report information, children learn to write in alternative formats; inviting and inspiring)

Improving Your Reading

REFERENCES

Using Reading Strategies

Irvin, Judith. *Reading and the Middle School Student: Strategies to Enhance Literacy*. Boston: Allyn and Bacon, 1990.

McNeil, John D. *Reading Comprehension: New Directions for Classroom Practice*. Chicago: Scott, Foresman, 1984.

Ogle, Donna. "KWL: A Teaching Model that Develops Active Reading of Expository Text." *The Reading Teacher* 39.1 (1986): 64-70.

Rosenblatt, Louise M. *Literature as Exploration*. New York: Modern Language Association, 1983.

RESOURCES

Brownlie, Faye, Susan Close, and Linda Wingren. *Tomorrow's Classroom Today: Strategies for Creating Active Readers, Writers, and Thinkers*. Portsmouth: Heinemann, 1990. (Current reading and writing strategies are carefully described.)

Docherty, Paul, ed. *The Visual Dictionary of the Universe*. New York: Houghton Mifflin, 1993. (Helps students think visually and provides teachers with good examples)

Grant, E. A. *Kids' Book of Secret Codes, Signals, & Ciphers*. Philadelphia: Running Press, 1989. (The book provides chapters on signals, sign languages, picture languages, and more. See "Picture Languages" for background information on, and examples of, hieroglyphs and hobo and Native American pictographs.)

McClure, Amy A., and Janice V. Kristo. *Inviting Children's Responses to Literature: Guides to 57 Notable Books*. Urbana: National Council of Teachers of English, 1994. (Offers ways to respond to notable books)

Routman, Regie. *Invitations: Changing as Teachers and Learners K-12*. Portsmouth: Heinemann, 1991. (A philosophically based text on teaching reading and writing across the curriculum with special chapters on at-risk populations, classroom management, and evaluation; contains a comprehensive reading list)

Improving Your Spelling and Vocabulary

REFERENCES

Building Vocabulary Skills

Nagy, William E. *Teaching Vocabulary to Improve Reading Comprehension*. Urbana: National Council of Teachers of English and International Reading Association, 1988.

Pittelman, Susan D., et al. *Semantic Feature Analysis: Classroom Application*. Newark: International Reading Association, 1991.

Becoming a Better Speller

Graves, Donald. *Writing: Teachers and Children at Work*. Portsmouth: Heinemann, 1983.

Temple, Charles. *The Beginnings of Writing*. 3rd ed. Boston: Allyn and Bacon, 1993.

RESOURCES

Bolton, Faye, and Diane Snowball. *Ideas for Spelling*. Portsmouth: Heinemann, 1993. (Spelling is dealt with in the context of writing in all areas of the curriculum.)

Cricket: The Magazine for Children. Mt. Morris: Carus Publishing. (Sidebars throughout this magazine highlight new vocabulary.)

Fry, Edward B. *New Reading Teacher's Book of Lists*. Englewood Cliffs: Prentice-Hall, 1985. (A jam-packed book of lists from A to Z on all aspects of the English language)

Gentry, J. Richard, and Jean W. Gillet. *Teaching Kids to Spell*. Portsmouth: Heinemann, 1993. (A good bridge between teachers working in traditional settings and whole language approaches)

Johnson, Dale D., and P. David Pearson. *Teaching Reading Vocabulary*. New York: Holt, Rinehart & Winston, 1978. (Provides specific strategies for improving vocabulary)

Marzano, Robert, and Jana Marzano. *A Cluster Approach to Elementary Vocabulary Instruction*. Newark: International Reading Association, 1988. (Discusses vocabulary building using superclusters of related words as a starting point)

Wilde, Sandra. *You Kan Red This! Spelling and Punctuation for Whole Language Classrooms, K-6*. Portsmouth: Heinemann, 1992. (A comprehensive and readable spelling handbook for teachers K-6)

Wood, Karen D., Diane Lapp, and James Flood. *Guiding Readers Through Text: A Review of Study Guides*. Newark: International Reading Association, 1992. (Seventeen of the most popular, effective reading study guides are presented by grade level in an easy-to-follow format.)

Improving Your Speaking and Listening

REFERENCES

Giving Speeches

Last, Ellen. *A Guide to Curriculum Planning in English Language Arts*. Madison: Wisconsin Department of Public Instruction, 1986.

Moffett, James, and Betty J. Wagner. *Student-Centered Language Arts, K-12*. Portsmouth: Heinemann, 1992.

Performing Poems

Wolf, Allan. *It's Show Time*. Ashville: Poetry Alive! Publications, 1993.

Improving Viewing Skills & Improving Listening Skills

Barchers, Suzanne I. *Teaching Language Arts: An Integrated Approach*. St. Paul: West Publishing, 1994.

RESOURCES

Wood, Karen D., Diane Lapp, and James Flood. "Collaborative Listening-Viewing Guide." *Guiding Readers Through Text: A Review of Study Guides*. Newark: International Reading Association, 1992. (Provides a framework for taking notes from information observed or heard)

Improving Your Thinking

REFERENCES

Thinking and Writing

Udall, Anne J., and Joan E. Daniels. *Creating the Thoughtful Classroom: Strategies to Promote Student Thinking*. Tucson: Zephyr Press, 1991.

Thinking Clearly

Costa, Arthur L. *Developing Minds, Vol. 1: A Resource Book for Teaching Thinking*. Assn. Supervision, 1991.

RESOURCES

Golub, Jeffrey N. *Activities to Promote Critical Thinking*. Urbana: National Council of Teachers of English, 1986. (Twenty-eight teacher-tested activities emphasize strengthening students' abilities to reason and to think clearly and critically.)

Golub, Jeffrey N. "The Great Junk Mail Project." *Activities for an Interactive Classroom*. Urbana: National Council of Teachers of English, 1994. (A powerful lesson on thinking clearly that involves helping students recognize doublespeak)

Kirby, Dan, and Carol Kuykendall. *Mind Matters: Teaching for Thinking*. Portsmouth: Heinemann, 1991. (Provides thoughtful habits of the mind for students)

Olson, Carol Booth. *Thinking Writing: Fostering Critical Thinking Through Writing*. New York: Harper Collins, 1992. (National Writing Project teachers offer a series of demonstration lessons that teach concrete strategies for integrating listening, speaking, reading, writing, and critical thinking across all grade levels.)

Improving Your Learning Skills

REFERENCES

Writing as a Learning Tool

Atwell, Nancie, ed. *Coming to Know: Writing to Learn in the Intermediate Grades*. Portsmouth: Heinemann, 1990.

Fulwiler, Toby, ed. *The Journal Book*. Portsmouth: Heinemann, 1987.

Working in Groups

Johnson, Roger T., et al. *Structuring Cooperative Learning: Lesson Plans for Teachers*. Interaction Book Company, 1987.

Taking Tests & Keeping Good Notes

Frender, Gloria. *Learning to Learn*. Nashville: Incentive Publications.

RESOURCES

Brooke, Robert, Ruth Mirtz, and Rick Evans. *Small Groups in Writing Workshops: Invitations to a Writer's Life*. Urbana: National Council of Teachers of English, 1994. (This is an inspirational book of narratives by teachers who take writing groups seriously. Many practical strategies are included.)

Harp, Bill, ed. *Assessment and Evaluation in Whole Language Programs*. Norwood: Christopher-Gordon, 1991. (One of the most comprehensive books today on assessment, in keeping with current thought on child development and learning—highly practical, as well)

Parsons, Les. *Response Journals*. Ontario: Pembroke Publishers Limited, 1990. (Provides a step-by-step system for establishing responsive writing as part of teaching, with many lists of possible prompts and criteria for assessment)

PLANNING NOTES

Reading/Writing Connection

RESOURCES

Butler, Andrea, and Jan Turbill. *Towards a Reading-Writing Classroom.* Portsmouth: Heinemann, 1987.

Crafton, Linda K. *Whole Language: Getting Started . . . Moving Forward.* Katonah: R. Owen, 1991.

Hansen, Jane, et al. *Breaking Ground: Teachers Relate Reading and Writing in the Elementary School.* Portsmouth: Heinemann, 1985.

Harste, Jerome, et al. *Creating Classrooms for Authors: The Reading-Writing Connection.* Portsmouth: Heinemann, 1988.

Harwayne, Shelley. *Lasting Impressions: Weaving Literature into the Writing Workshop.* Portsmouth: Heinemann, 1992.

Writing Across the Curriculum

RESOURCES

Braddon, Kathryn L., et al., eds. *Math Through Children's Literature: Making the NCTM Standards Come Alive.* Englewood: Teacher Idea Press, 1993.

Butzow, Carol M., and John W. Butzow. *Science Through Children's Literature.* Englewood: Teacher Idea Press, 1989.

Tchudi, Stephen, ed. *The Astonishing Curriculum: Integrating Science and Humanities Through Language.* Urbana: National Council of Teachers of English, 1993.

Tchudi, Stephen, and Susan Tchudi. *Teaching Writing in the Content Areas: Elementary School.* Washington: National Education Association, 1983.

Thias, Christopher. *Language Across the Curriculum in the Elementary Grades.* Urbana: National Council of Teachers of English, 1986.

Students with Special Needs

RESOURCES

Five, Cora L. *Special Voices.* Portsmouth: Heinemann, 1992.

Law, Barbara, and Mary Eckes. *The More Than Just Surviving Handbook: ESL for Every Classroom Teacher.* Winnipeg, Canada: Peguis, 1990.

Rhodes, Lynn K., and Curt Dudley-Marling. *Readers and Writers with a Difference: A Holistic Approach to Teaching Learning Disabled and Remedial Students.* Portsmouth: Heinemann, 1988.

Spangenberg-Urbschat, Karen, and Robert Pritchard, eds. *Kids Come in All Languages: Reading Instruction for ESL Students.* Newark: International Reading Association, 1994.

Language Series Overview

This section provides an overview of the ***Writers Express Language Series***, the program of activities for grades 4 and 5 that coordinates with the student handbook. Of special interest to you will be the introduction to the Language Series on page 186 and the overview of activities that follows on pages 187-191. This section concludes with a closer look at various program activities.

Introducing . . .

A Closer Look at the . . .

The Complete *Writers Express* Program

There are four main components in the program: (1) the ***Writers Express*** student handbook; (2) the ***Writers Express Teacher's Guide;*** (3) the ***Writers Express Language Series Program Guide*** for each grade level, 4-5; and (4) the ***Writers Express SourceBook*** of activities for each grade level, 4-5. Here's how the different components can work in your classroom:

The **Writers Express** handbook serves as students' core resource for writing, thinking, and learning.

The **Writers Express Teacher's Guide** provides basic planning ideas, start-up activities, and minilessons.

The **Writers Express Language Series Program Guide** (one for each grade level, 4-5) provides everything you need to teach this comprehensive program including planning notes and blackline masters for each chapter in the handbook, a suggested yearlong timetable of lessons, and evaluating guidelines for the program activities—all in one ring binder.

The **Writers Express SourceBook** (one for each grade level, 4-5) provides activities addressing basic language and proofreading skills.

The Process of Writing

	Type of Activity	Grade Level
Getting Started		
All About Writing	Basic Unit	4 and 5
One Writer's Process	Basic Unit	4 and 5
A Basic Writing Guide	Basic Unit	4 and 5
Writing with a Computer	Basic Unit	4 and 5
Planning Your Portfolio	Basic Unit	4 and 5
Prewriting and Drafting Guide		
Prewriting and Drafting Guide	Basic Unit	4 and 5
Building a File of Writing Ideas	Writer's Workshop	4 and 5
Selecting a Subject	Writer's Workshop	4 and 5
Starting Points for Writing	Writer's Workshop	4 and 5
Collecting Details	Writer's Workshop	4 and 5
Planning and Drafting Tips	Writer's Workshop	4 and 5
Building a Resource of Writing Forms	Writer's Workshop	4 and 5
Revising and Editing Guide		
Revising Your Writing	Basic Unit	4 and 5
Conferencing with Partners	Basic Unit	4 and 5
Sharing Family Stories	Extended Unit	4 and 5
Editing and Proofreading	Basic Unit	4 and 5
Publishing Your Writing	Basic Unit	4 and 5
Building Paragraphs and Essays		
Writing Paragraphs	Basic Unit	4 and 5
Writing Essays	Extended Unit	4 and 5
A Writing Sampler	Basic Unit	4 and 5
Improving Your Writing Skills		
Writing Basic Sentences	Basic Unit	4 and 5
Combining Sentences	Basic Unit	4 and 5
Modeling the Masters	Extended Unit	4 and 5

The Forms of Writing

	Type of Activity	Grade Level
Personal Writing		
Writing in Journals	Basic Unit	4 and 5
Writing Personal Narratives	Extended Unit	4 and 5
Writing Friendly Letters	Extended Unit	4 and 5
Subject Writing		
Writing Newspaper Stories	Extended Unit	5
Writing Book Reviews	Extended Unit	4 and 5
Writing Explanations	Extended Unit	4
Writing Business Letters	Extended Unit	5
Writing Observation Reports	Extended Unit	4
Writing Tales and Stories		
Writing Fantasies	Extended Unit	5
Writing Tall Tales	Extended Unit	4
Writing Realistic Stories	Extended Unit	4
Writing Stories from History	Extended Unit	5
Writing Poems, Plays, and Songs		
Writing Poems	Extended Unit	4 and 5
Writing Songs	Extended Unit	5
Writing Plays	Extended Unit	4
Writing Riddles	Extended Unit	5
Writing for Fun	Basic Unit	4 and 5
Research Writing		
Using the Library	Basic Unit	4 and 5
Writing a Summary	Extended Unit	4 and 5
Writing a Classroom Report	Extended Unit	5

The Tools of Learning

	Type of Activity	Grade Level
Improving Your Reading		
Using Reading Strategies	Extended Unit	4 and 5
Reading Pictures	Basic Unit	4 and 5
Improving Your Spelling and Vocabulary		
Building Vocabulary Skills	Basic Unit	4 and 5
Becoming a Better Speller	Basic Unit	4 and 5
Improving Your Speaking and Listening		
Giving Speeches	Extended Unit	5
Performing Poems	Extended Unit	4
Improving Viewing Skills	Basic Unit	4 and 5
Improving Listening Skills	Basic Unit	4 and 5
Improving Your Thinking		
Getting Organized	Basic Unit	4 and 5
Thinking and Writing	Basic Unit	4 and 5
Thinking Clearly	Basic Unit	4 and 5
Improving Your Learning Skills		
Writing as a Learning Tool	Basic Unit	4 and 5
Completing Assignments	Basic Unit	4 and 5
Working in Groups	Basic Unit	4 and 5
Taking Tests	Basic Unit	4 and 5
Keeping Good Notes	Basic Unit	4 and 5

Proofreader's Guide

	Type of Activity	Grade Level
Marking Punctuation		
End Punctuation, Commas		4 and 5
Appositives		5
Commas and Clauses		4 and 5
Commas and End Punctuation Review		4 and 5
Apostrophes		4 and 5
Possessives		4
Quotation Marks		4 and 5
Semicolons, Hyphens, Punctuating Titles		5
Italics, Parentheses, Punctuation Review		5
Editing for Mechanics		
Capitalization, Plurals		4 and 5
Numbers, Abbreviations		4 and 5
Checking Your Spelling		
Checking Your Spelling		4 and 5
Using the Right Word		
Using the Right Word		4 and 5
Understanding Sentences		
Sentence Variety		4 and 5
Sentence Problems		4 and 5
Sentence Combining		4 and 5
Understanding Our Language		
Nouns, Pronouns, Verbs		4 and 5
Adjectives, Adverbs		4 and 5
Other Parts of Speech		4 and 5

The basic skills listed on this page are covered in practice workshops, minilessons, and/or daily sentences found in the SourceBook.

The Student Almanac

	Type of Activity	Grade Level
Useful Tables and Lists		
Useful Tables and Lists	Basic Unit	4 and 5
Sign Language	Minilessons	4 and 5
Foreign Words	Minilessons	4 and 5
Animal Facts	Minilessons	4 and 5
Metric System	Minilessons	4 and 5
Conversion Table	Minilessons	4 and 5
Planet Profiles	Minilessons	4 and 5
Using Maps		
Using Maps	Extended Unit/Minilesson	4 and 5
Improving Math Skills		
Improving Math Skills	Basic Unit	4 and 5
Solving Word Problems	Minilessons	4 and 5
Symbols	Minilessons	4 and 5
Roman Numerals	Minilessons	4 and 5
History in the Making		
History in the Making	Basic Unit	4 and 5
The U.S. Constitution	Minilessons	4 and 5
U.S. Presidents	Minilessons	4 and 5
Historical Time Line	Minilessons	4 and 5

A Closer Look at the Writing Units: Chapter Notes

■ **The chapter notes will help you implement the writing units in the program. This overview explains how these units work.**

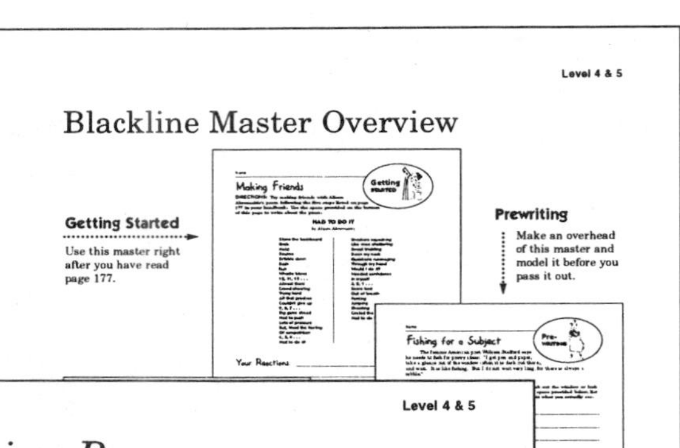
Level 4 & 5

Blackline Master Overview

Getting Started

Use this master right after you have read page 177.

Prewriting

Make an overhead of this master and model it before you pass it out.

3. Overview Page

Provides facsimiles of the blackline masters plus tips for implementation

1. Introductory Page

Discusses the handbook chapter and provides planning notes

Level 4 & 5

Writing Poems

(pages 177-187)

Introduction — *Writing Poems* begins with an invitation to make friends with poetry. Anne-Marie Oomen then invites students to think about what makes poetry special. After this puzzle is solved, students are guided through the steps for writing free-verse poetry. The chapter continues with definitions and examples of figures of speech and poetic devices for creating effective images and sounds in poetry. Finally, helpful lists of traditional and invented poetry types are provided.

Rationale

- ■ *Writing poetry gives students an opportunity to better understand this form of writing.*
- ■ *Writing poetry offers students a personal and creative avenue for exploring and expressing their ideas.*
- ■ *Students learn to choose words purposefully.*
- ■ *Students come to understand that sounds of words and figures of speech help to convey meaning.*

Major Concepts

- ☐ **Poets often speak from personal experience.** (pages 177-180)
- ☐ **The language of poetry is keen and alive.** (page 181)
- ☐ **Poets often use figures of speech.** (page 182)
- ☐ **The sound of poetry is important.** (page 183)
- ☐ **There are many types of poems.** (pages 184-187)

Planning Notes — RELATED MATERIALS: Because this chapter introduces many types of poems, having examples of poems visible in the classroom will nurture student curiosity.

2. Express to the Handbook

Presents step-by-step implementation guidelines

4. Special Planning Notes in Extended Units

Offer additional planning ideas, including special-needs notes and writing options

Level 4 & 5

EXPRESS TO THE HANDBOOK

The "Express to the Handbook" notes and coordinating blackline masters are designed to help your students write a free-verse poem.

Getting Started (pages 177-179)

The chapter opens in a hands-on fashion with little talk and lots of "doing." Anne-Marie Oomen, a poet and our major contributor to this chapter, invites students to make friends with poetry right away. Then she explains what makes a poem—a poem.

Option 1: After making friends with Oomen's poem "Words" (page 177), pass out the blackline master "Getting Started," and work with the poem "Had to Do It." You may also use this same poem as you discuss "What Is Poetry?" on pages 178 and 179 in the handbook.

Option 2: Use page 177 and the blackline master as stated above. Then ask your students, "What is poetry?" Have them respond in their notebooks. Then read pages 178 and 179 in the handbook. Compare and discuss our answers with the students' answers.

Prewriting (page 180)

With your students, read the prewriting section on page 180. Then give your students the blackline master "Prewriting." Discuss William Stafford's quote and read over the directions for the listing activity. After the students write their lists, ask them to free-write, just as Oomen did on page 180 in the handbook.

Writing the First Draft (page 180)

Once your students have finished their free writing, pass out the blackline master "Writing the First Draft." The master gives a step-by-step way to turn their free writing into poetry. Once they have done this, encourage the students to add, take out, and rewrite words, phrases, even lines.

Revising (pages 181-183)

Jeffrey Copland, author of *Speaking of Poets*, has interviewed many poets over the years and found "all [of them] mentioned the revision process was a true joy." It can be the same for your students as they learn to make every word count.

To help children "show" instead of "tell," use the blackline master "Revising the Writing." Pages 181-182 in the handbook will help them add word pictures to their poems; page 183 will help them improve the sound of their poems.

Traditional and Invented Poetry (pages 184-187)

In addition to teaching free verse in this chapter, we have listed many other types of poems and included many examples. Have students use the handbook to identify the poems they enjoy, by type. Also share poetry books with the class, and identify poetry types together.

102 *Writing Poems*

Level 4 & 5

Special Planning Notes

MINI LESSON — For those children who just can't get off square one with poetry, here's a good idea to get them started. Have them write a short bio-poem to introduce a close friend, a family member, a famous individual, or perhaps a character from a book. Follow this model:

Eleanor
First Lady
A symbol of goodwill
Who's Who in America and around the world
Woman
Who made a difference
Roosevelt

EXPRESS TO STUDENTS WITH SPECIAL NEEDS

Students with special needs will benefit from reading poetry, lots of it, before being asked to write it. In addition, teachers with an ear for poetic thought can help special-needs students turn their ideas into poetry. For example, student Soo Young, a recent immigrant, made a profound connection between his country and his new home: "My home, this country looks like stars in the sky back home." When asked to explain, he said, "Lights all over." This thought prompted the following poem:

My home, this country,
Like stars in the sky back home.
Lights all over.

Other-Grade **OPTION** — Your students will enjoy turning fables into rhyme, and this gives you a perfect opportunity to introduce fables from other countries. English-speaking children think of Aesop's fables, but your French children will think of La Fontaine. Oriental students will know the fables of Bidpai or the Jatakos. Native American children might know *Dr. Coyote: A Native American Aesop's Fable* by John Bierhorst.

To introduce your students to rhymed versions of fables, read to them from *Aesop's Fables: Retold in Verse* by Tom Paxton.

108 *Writing Poems*

Blackline Masters

■ **Unit masters address different stages in the development of the students' writing. The type and number of masters vary from unit to unit.**

Getting Started

Name

Making Friends

Getting STARTED

DIRECTIONS: Try making friends with Alison Abromaitis's poem following the five steps listed on page 177 in your handbook. Use the space provided on the bottom of this page to write about the poem.

HAD TO DO IT

by Alison Abromaitis

Slams the backboard
Grab
Hold
Bounce
Dribble down
Dash
Run
Whistle blows

Sneakers squeaking
Like mice chattering
Sweat trickling
Down my neck
Questions rummaging
Through my head
Would I do it?
Needed confidence

Your Reacti

104 *Writing Poem*

Prewriting

Name

Fishing for a Subject

Pre-WRITING

The famous American poet William Stafford says he needs to fish for poetry ideas: "I get pen and paper, take a glance out of the window (often it is dark out there), and wait. It is like fishing. But I do not wait very long, for there is always a nibble."

DIRECTIONS: To think of ideas for your own poem, look out the window or look toward a place in the room that you like. Then in the space provided below, list all the ideas that come to mind, even ideas not related to what you actually see.

r thoughts

Jow, on your own paper, wri
on't worry about correct s
on paper. (For a sample fr
your handbook.)

Writing the First Draft

Name

Creating a Poem

WRITING THE First Draft

DIRECTIONS: Follow the steps below to turn your free writing into the first draft of a poem.

Step 1: Read your free writing out loud—twice.

Step 2: On the second reading, wherever you take a breath or slow down, draw a slash mark (/).

Example: I knew if I dropped the flag / I would die. / I knew if a corner of the flag touched the ground / I would die. / I knew if a corner of the flag touched the ground / the friend I was folding it with / would die, too!

Step 3: Then begin shaping your poem by starting a new line after each slash.

Example: I knew if I dropped the flag
I would die.
I knew if a corner of the flag touched the ground
I would die.
I knew if a corner of the flag touched the ground
the friend I was folding it with
would die, too!

Use the space below to rewrite your poem according to your slash marks.

Step 4: Once you have made all your line breaks, carefully study the first draft of your poem. You may want to try moving words (or parts) around. You may also want to add or change some words.

106 *Writing Poems*

Revising the Writing

Name

Improving Your Poem

Revising THE WRITING

DIRECTIONS: Use the following checklist as a guide when you review and revise your poem. (You can also use this checklist to review your classmates' poetry.)

_____ **1. Add word pictures.**
Make sure your action words give a clear picture. For example, Anne-Marie Oomen chose to use "tossed" rather than "handed" in her model poem (page 181 in the handbook) because "tossed" created a better picture.

_____ **2. Check for pleasing sounds.**
Sounds make a poem more interesting to read, and sometimes more fun to hear. In the lines below, the poet paid attention to his consonant and vowel sounds.

The tires zipped against the ice,
whining like a line of bees buzzing home.

_____ **3. Watch for chances to make special comparisons.**
The underlined similes (a *simile* is a type of comparison) add special meaning to the following lines from the model poem:

I tossed him half my butter sandwich
and he danced like loose litter in wind.
And once I climbed
slow as an
old fly
down our fire escape

(See "Figures of Speech" on page 182 for examples of other types of special comparisons.)

_____ **4. Think about the arrangement of the lines in your poem.**
Do all the line breaks add meaning to your poem? And does the poem look interesting or fun? Study other poems for ideas.

Writing Poems 107

A Closer Look at the Practice Workshops

At each grade level, there are more than 60 workshops designed to provide basic skills instruction and practice. Each workshop provides a user-friendly, self-contained unit of work.

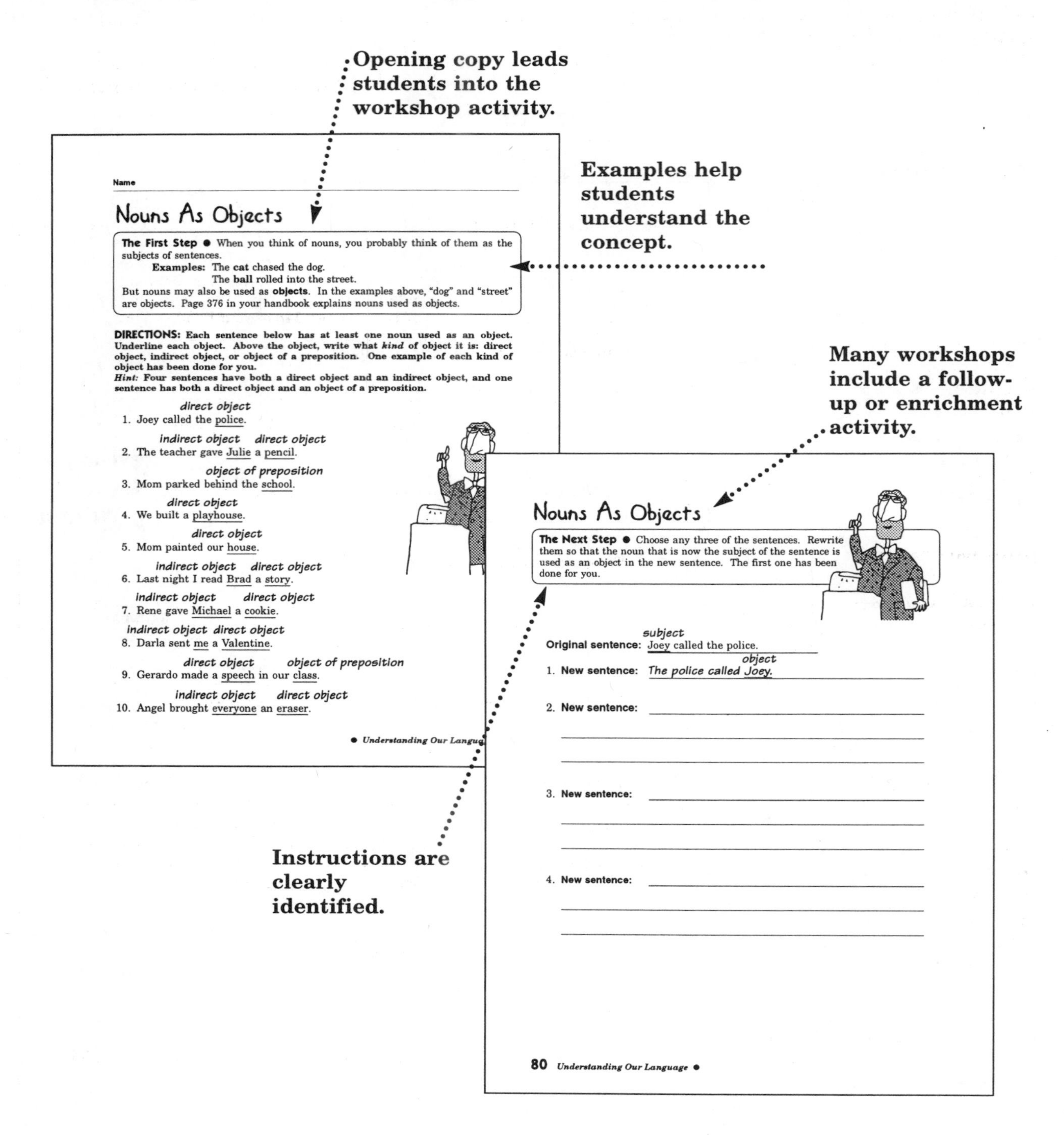

Name

Nouns As Objects

The First Step ● When you think of nouns, you probably think of them as the subjects of sentences.

Examples: The **cat** chased the dog.
The **ball** rolled into the street.

But nouns may also be used as **objects**. In the examples above, "dog" and "street" are objects. Page 376 in your handbook explains nouns used as objects.

DIRECTIONS: Each sentence below has at least one noun used as an object. Underline each object. Above the object, write what *kind* of object it is: direct object, indirect object, or object of a preposition. One example of each kind of object has been done for you.
***Hint:* Four sentences have both a direct object and an indirect object, and one sentence has both a direct object and an object of a preposition.**

1. Joey called the police. (*direct object*)
2. The teacher gave Julie a pencil. (*indirect object*, *direct object*)
3. Mom parked behind the school. (*object of preposition*)
4. We built a playhouse. (*direct object*)
5. Mom painted our house. (*direct object*)
6. Last night I read Brad a story. (*indirect object*, *direct object*)
7. Rene gave Michael a cookie. (*indirect object*, *direct object*)
8. Darla sent me a Valentine. (*indirect object*, *direct object*)
9. Gerardo made a speech in our class. (*direct object*, *object of preposition*)
10. Angel brought everyone an eraser. (*indirect object*, *direct object*)

● *Understanding Our Langua*

Nouns As Objects

The Next Step ● Choose any three of the sentences. Rewrite them so that the noun that is now the subject of the sentence is used as an object in the new sentence. The first one has been done for you.

Original sentence: Joey called the police. (*subject*: Joey)

1. **New sentence:** *The police called Joey.* (*object*: Joey)
2. **New sentence:** ______
3. **New sentence:** ______
4. **New sentence:** ______

80 *Understanding Our Language* ●

Minilessons

There are minilessons at each grade level that address usage, mechanics, and grammar questions covered in the "Proofreader's Guide." There are other minilessons that focus on information about maps, charts, math, and the historical time line found in "The Student Almanac."

Opening copy leads students directly into the minilesson.

Some minilessons include examples to help students understand a concept.

Many minilessons can be reproduced as quick activity sheets.

Some minilessons direct students to references in addition to their handbooks.

The frog caught the fly—ZAP! . . . . *Dashes*

To each of the following sentences, ADD the word or phrase that appears next to it. Set off the added words with dashes. (Remember, dashes show a quick change in direction or an interruption in the flow of thought.) An example has been done for you. Also see **page 348** of your handbook.

1. A frog landed right in my lap. **plop!**

   A frog landed—plop!—right in my lap.

2. My little sister jumped out the window. **she was born goofy**

   ____

3. I finished my homework and went to bed. **at last**

   ____

4. The alarm clock went off at 6:00 a.m. **RINGGG!!!**

   ____

5. She slammed the door and yelled at me. **BANG!**

   ____

6. School will be out for the summer in three days. **hooray!**

   ____

What's does it mean? . . . . *Apostrophe*

WRITE the word or phrase that each of the following contractions represents. CHECK your work by looking up each contraction in the dictionary. Then, on your own paper, USE the contractions in sentences. You may use more than one contraction in each sentence. Also see **page 349** in your handbook.

1. I'll ______________
2. it's ______________
3. doesn't ______________
4. we'd ______________
5. they're ______________
6. haven't ______________

Marking Punctuation Minilessons **109**

A Closer Look at the Check-It-Out Daily Sentences

The Check-It-Out Daily Sentences at each grade level come in two varieties. In the focused sentences, students concentrate on one proofreading skill at a time. For example, one week's worth of sentences focuses exclusively on using commas in a series. (See the example below.) In the proofreading sentences, students check sentences containing two or three different types of errors.

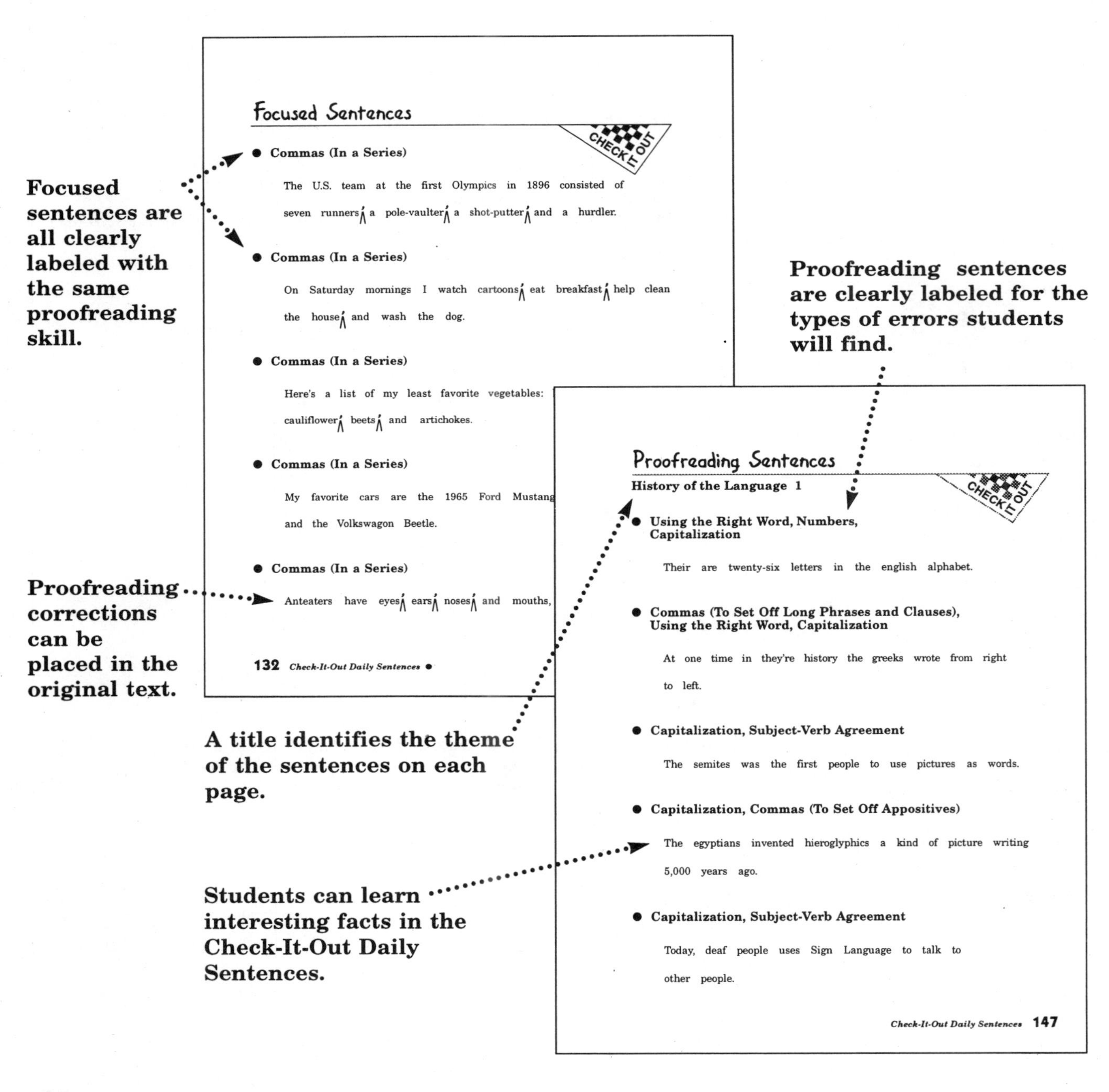

Focused Sentences

- **Commas (In a Series)**

  The U.S. team at the first Olympics in 1896 consisted of seven runners, a pole-vaulter, a shot-putter, and a hurdler.

- **Commas (In a Series)**

  On Saturday mornings I watch cartoons, eat breakfast, help clean the house, and wash the dog.

- **Commas (In a Series)**

  Here's a list of my least favorite vegetables: cauliflower, beets, and artichokes.

- **Commas (In a Series)**

  My favorite cars are the 1965 Ford Mustang and the Volkswagon Beetle.

- **Commas (In a Series)**

  Anteaters have eyes, ears, noses, and mouths,

132 *Check-It-Out Daily Sentences* ●

Proofreading Sentences

History of the Language 1

- **Using the Right Word, Numbers, Capitalization**

  Their are twenty-six letters in the english alphabet.

- **Commas (To Set Off Long Phrases and Clauses), Using the Right Word, Capitalization**

  At one time in they're history the greeks wrote from right to left.

- **Capitalization, Subject-Verb Agreement**

  The semites was the first people to use pictures as words.

- **Capitalization, Commas (To Set Off Appositives)**

  The egyptians invented hieroglyphics a kind of picture writing 5,000 years ago.

- **Capitalization, Subject-Verb Agreement**

  Today, deaf people uses Sign Language to talk to other people.

Check-It-Out Daily Sentences **147**